Nichetto Studio
Projects, Collaborations and Conversations in Design

NICHETTO STUDIO
PROJECTS
COLLABORATIONS
AND CONVERSATIONS
IN DESIGN

Φ

7 *Nichetto Studio,* Max Fraser

9 *The Formative Years: Italian Design and the Increasing Complexity of Globalization,* Francesca Picchi

14–231 Projects 001–137

233 Index

19	*Defining a New Italian Design Language* Eero Koivisto in conversation with Max Fraser
27	Project 137: Steinway & Sons, Gran Nichetto
39	*The Great Matchmaker* Robert Polan in conversation with Max Fraser
47	Project 133: Ginori 1735, LCDC Collection
57	*Porcelain Never Forgets* Alessandro Badii in conversation with Francesca Picchi
65	Project 096: Sancal, Next Stop
75	*No Stitching in Upholstery* Marie-Louise Rosholm in conversation with Francesca Picchi
83	Project 084: Hermès, Pure Imagination
95	*Getting Close to the Culture* Yoko Choy in conversation with Max Fraser
103	Project 073: Salviati, Pyrae/Strata
113	*The Origin: Murano and Glassmaking* Dario Stellon in conversation with Francesca Picchi
121	Luca Nichetto: Four Interviews with Max Fraser
137	*Design is a Good Way to Get in Touch with our Fellow Women and Men* Beatrice Leanza in conversation with Francesca Picchi
145	Project 047: ZaoZuo Collection
155	*Pushing Across Boundaries* Shu Wei in conversation with Max Fraser
163	Project 038: Nichetto = nendo
173	*Dialogue, Collaboration and Laughter* Oki Sato in conversation with Max Fraser
181	Project 033: Cassina, La Mise
191	*Design is All About Proportions* Ferdinando Mussi in conversation with Francesca Picchi
199	Project 028: Foscarini, Plass
209	*Think of a Region Like a Huge Factory* Loris Tessaro in conversation with Francesca Picchi
217	Project 020: Offecct, Robo
227	*Looking Outside the Small Garden of Italian Design* Francesco Dompieri in conversation with Max Fraser

Nichetto Studio, Max Fraser

Luca Nichetto nearly became a basketball player, dribbling, shooting and slam-dunking his way to a professional level at the age of sixteen. But the sweaty basketball court had competition from the scorching furnaces of Murano, the centuries-old centre of Italian glass where he grew up. His grandfather was a master glassblower and Luca was forever fascinated by his ability to transform the toffee-like molten substance into exquisite forms, layered with expertise and awareness of heritage.

Witnessing the transformation of a drawing into an object became a natural part of Luca's upbringing, so much so that he and his friends would tour the factories of Murano, knocking on the doors and selling their drawings, earning pocket money to see them through their teenage summers. Indeed, Luca was all about having fun, an attitude he maintains to this day.

This exposure to the artistic expression of the glass industry around him was a strong signal that one could convert one's passion into a living, presenting Luca with a dilemma – would his pursuit be bouncy balls or gleaming glass? That decision was to decide his future.

Luca doesn't profess to have chosen to become a designer – it was a natural development from his exposure to the world around him as a child, where ninety per cent of the people in his life were involved in the glass market. He was keen to stay in Venice and picked the Industrial Design course at the Istituto Universitario di Architettura di Venezia (IUAV), where he became known as the 'Glass Boy' by his peers and professors for regularly converting his student ideas into the medium with which he was familiar and had access. At the same time, he turned away from professional basketball when it was no longer fun, instead playing the game at a local level and preferring to focus on his studies and this thing called Design.

The first decade of Luca's working life mostly centred on Italy, and his loyalty to Venice and the wider industrial base of the Veneto region remained true. Many suppliers and expert manufacturers were accessible within an hour of Venice, garnering relationships for the new designer that would prove crucial to establishing his local network. The allure of the design capital of Milan never tempted Luca; he was spurred along in those early years by a pride for his locality and a resistance to the 'design club' of Milan as well as a happy-go-lucky attitude and a desire to follow his instincts.

While Venice might have been his epicentre and his life was arguably quite insular as a result, international basketball competitions throughout his teens had nevertheless given him a taster of the outside world. Tournaments had taken him to cities such as Chicago where he competed against international teams. As much as he was happy on his home turf, Luca always had an open mind to the opportunities elsewhere, an attitude that would prove fruitful as his career unfolded.

Before long, Luca realized that he would need to spread his wings outside Italy and that prospects were beckoning from foreign shores. In the end it was his personal life, not solely his profession, that led him to Sweden. His Swedish partner, Åsa, had a job offer that led her to return to her native country, and Luca followed her. By no means was he turning his back on Italy, rather he was inspired by the international approach of his peers from other countries; if they could appeal to brands in Italy, then surely he could do the same elsewhere.

Some erratic English, plenty of sign language and several prototypes later, Luca was standing at the gates of a new era for his studio and one that would send clear signals to his generation of Italian designers that, despite the mature nature of the Italian design scene and its global reputation, it is not the only territory for a native to explore. Inadvertently, by casting his net into Sweden in 2010 he grew more exotic in his own country, gaining several new Italian clients as well as attracting producers in other countries worldwide. In the space of a few years, Luca and the studio team were undertaking furniture and product-design commissions, interiors, exhibitions and art direction for large and small companies across a variety of nations including the United Kingdom, France, Spain, Portugal, Germany, Finland, Russia and Canada, as well as in the behemoths of China and the United States.

That repertoire has continued to evolve, culminating in more than 400 products and projects over two decades and counting. This book celebrates an edited selection of 137, sharing the sketches and prototypes as much as the finished objects. Luca focuses on ten of these projects as case studies, reporting on some of the challenges as well as the significance of those assignments to the development of his practice.

But the projects don't come without the people, and this book is also a celebration of some of the individuals who have, for one reason or another, played a defining role along Luca's journey. Of all the characters who have touched his life, this volume includes conversations with a dozen people who have left a lasting impression on Luca, those who have trusted in him, who have given him a leg up at pivotal moments and sustain their relationship to this day. My co-author and I were keen to include their voices, quizzing them on the formation of their relationship, asking for their impressions of Luca's trajectory, as well as probing their opinions on the state of the design industry and the climate in which Nichetto Studio operates.

Luca is always the first to acknowledge the steady flow of talented people with whom his life overlaps and with whom he toils, confides, discusses and, importantly, laughs. Perhaps most notable are his background heroes, the talented individuals who have passed through his studio and, of course, those who are currently seated next to him.

Over the years that we've known each other, Luca and I have often had very honest chats about the state of the design industry, during which we have acknowledged great work, chastised the superfluous and gossiped over industry rumours and controversy. Luca has never shied away from his opinions and has always preserved his good humour. During the development of this book, I had the privilege of spending several hours in discussion with Luca via video calls during the Covid-19 pandemic. Across several sessions, we would tackle a macro topic such as 'sustainability' or 'education', and I tried to allow the conversations to meander as naturally as possible. The essence of what was said has been published in this book (see pages 121– 132), giving you a flavour of Luca's thoughts on the design business and the wider society in which he operates today.

Regardless of the topic, a recurring feature of our discussions was laughter as Luca fondly recalled stories from his past, rarely taking himself too seriously or hyping the beat of his own drum. His humility is refreshing, his willingness to admit when he isn't sure is direct, and his ability to laugh at himself is admirable.

One of Luca's core attributes is his curiosity, and when this combines with his somewhat happy-go-lucky attitude to life, there is no conversation he isn't willing to have. This appetite for new adventures has unlocked countless opportunities and dialogues that have manifested through the varied output of his burgeoning studio over two decades. He would claim not to be tactical and, whether you believe that or not, his strategy of non-strategy has allowed him to transcend territories, challenge his own comfort levels, convince others to take him on their journey and form lasting relationships along the way.

Max Fraser is the author of multiple design books including *Design UK*, *London Design Guide* and *Designers on Design*, which he co-wrote with Sir Terence Conran, he also contributes to publications including the *Financial Times*, *Wallpaper**, *icon*, *Surface*, *London's Evening Standard*, *CNN* and *Newsweek International*. He is a curator of design exhibitions and events in the UK and abroad. As a consultant, he delivers content and strategy for a variety of public and private bodies including MINI, Dassault Systèmes, Norwegian Embassy, Offecct, Hermès, Dubai Design Week, 100% Design, Clerkenwell Design Week and London Design Festival.

*The Formative Years: Italian Design
and the Increasing Complexity of Globalization*,
Francesca Picchi

Luca Nichetto started building his reputation as an international designer on Murano, the island in the Venetian lagoon where he was born in 1976. His family has always lived on Murano; his grandfather was a skilled glassblower and the Murano glassmakers and their community formed the setting for Luca's early work as a designer when he was a young student of industrial design at IUAV. At that time he was trying to imagine how to make his own contribution in a field with such an exemplary history as Italian design, where tradition hardly seemed to leave much room for innovation. This same feeling, of being overwhelmed by the weight of history, was common to the generation of designers that followed the golden age of Italian design, that of the masters who emerged in the post-war period.

In the years of far-reaching changes that accompanied Nichetto's training, the watchword was internationalization. The new millennium was significantly overshadowed by the great financial crisis that struck in 2007 and the ensuing recession of 2008–2009, triggering the most serious economic crisis since the Great Depression of 1929. Such upheaval presented the industry with a life-or-death choice: to change or succumb, the constant condition of existence.

Just as the economic turbulence was looming on the horizon, Nichetto took up the profession of industrial designer following his early success with glassware. His first project, the Millebolle vase for Salviati (2000, see page 14), became a bestseller for one of the most renowned Venetian glassmaking firms as soon as it appeared on the market. After this successful beginning, in 2006 Nichetto opened his own project and design consultancy, Nichetto & Partners, in Porto Marghera. A city on the mainland close to Venice, it is one of Italy's biggest industrial districts, with a commercial port and manufacturing hub.

At the time, together with the crisis in major industry, economic observers in Italy recorded a significant growth in the number of small and medium-sized businesses. Although their progress was fragmented and uncertain, they appeared determined to follow ethical paths to growth by innovating and developing internationally.

This dynamism seems to have been particularly evident in the Veneto, a region of Italy that displayed remarkable signs of vitality amid the general crisis. It was there that Nichetto was born and worked. His contacts with the region's production system, notable for its readiness to experiment and innovate, was the school that prompted him to take up design. He started from glass with its economic ecosystem based on a material culture with a glorious tradition, an archive of unmatched models and production skills that were unique worldwide. The industry, however, had lost some of its innovative force, lapsing into the repetition of traditional models.

In this scenario, with its indefinite, shifting outlines driven by the need for interconnection within an increasingly complex and constantly changing market, Nichetto started working as a designer in Venice. The city had a solid reputation in the field, but it was essentially an outlier compared to Milan, the capital around which the Italian design community gravitates.

When Nichetto was at the start of his career, the Triennale di Milano (an outstanding showcase for Italian design) opened its first "mutant" design museum. It was conceived in keeping with a changing vision that meant it would be renewed each year. The "scientific curator" of the first edition of the museum was Andrea Branzi, a master of Italian design, a leading member of the Radical movement and one of the founders of the Memphis group with Ettore Sottsass.

It was Branzi himself who set the goal of mapping and promoting the work and talent of the new generations by organizing a systematic exploration of what he termed 'a region whose boundaries are hard to trace'. One of the questions he started from was: 'How to imagine producing a hundred thousand Achille Castiglionis?' In this spirit the Triennale launched the exhibition *The New Italian Design. Il paesaggio mobile del nuovo design italiano* (literally: the changing landscape of the new Italian design). Described as a 'census', it aimed to conduct a survey of a new generation of designers active in contemporary Italy.

In his analysis, Branzi noted that, despite the crisis, the number of designers had grown surprisingly, making design 'the most typical mass profession of the twenty-first century'. He also observed that design had undergone a mutation and from being a unique, decisive act had developed into what he described as an 'enzymatic swarming behaviour involving countless players'. He concluded: 'Comparison with the age of the masters is pointless. No one needs masterpieces, meaning definitive products. Rather we need strategies capable of continuously turning out new products, new services, new promotions, new communications. Dynamic energies that will enable businesses to cope with international competition and the new globalized markets.'

Branzi's analysis of the changes that were taking place was indeed brilliant, but not all the participants in the exhibition wholly appreciated his reading of the situation. They felt somehow underestimated by an interpretation that tended to confuse their identity as designers in a featureless swarm. And the 'gaseous' state of design was exemplified by a selection of exhibits that contained a prevalence of 'furnishings bordering on the superfluous', intended to confirm this thesis.

Nichetto was among the young designers selected, being represented by a set of objects that included a one-piece lamp produced with the cutting-edge technology of injection-moulded silicone. Called Jerry, the lamp was developed in conjunction with Casamania, a Venetian company that was giving commissions to young designers as it sought to build a reputation and position itself in the market. Since the product implied expertise and substantial investment in terms of moulds, Nichetto and Casamania persuaded a company expert in making cake moulds to move into this new field.

In this early period, Nichetto worked not only with important brands with a solid reputation in glassmaking, but also with young Venetian companies striving to expand on the market through design. They included Foscarini, a lighting company set up on Murano in 1981 with the idea of exploiting blown glass. It later moved to the mainland to experiment with new technology. Nichetto completed an internship with this young company while he was still a student, and that led to his appointment from 2001 to 2003 as consultant for research into new materials and product development. While working in the factory he devised some iconic products, including the Plass lamp (2011, see page 45), which tested the polycarbonate rotomoulding technique for the first time in the field of domestic lighting and revealed some constants of Nichetto's work. These include the leap in scale, the transfer of technology and a marked sensibility in dealing with plastic materials to bring out their latent qualities of modulating and filtering light, a result of the sensibility he had acquired through working with glass. Finally, these products reflected a certain curiosity that prompted him to explore generally neglected industrial fields and experiment with cheap techniques for the sake of affordable industrial production.

At this point I would like to make a brief personal digression. The first time I heard of Luca Nichetto was in April 2008 in Milan. This was during the Salone del Mobile, with its typical whirl of events attracting hundreds of thousands of visitors, and hotel beds at a premium. I used to call daily on the designer Giulio Iacchetti in his studio while we were working on an exhibition that the new Museum of Design at the Triennale had decided to organize to promote the work of young Italian designers, helping them to emerge from the shadow of the masters. The general feeling was that Italian design would be in troubled straits if no one invested in the new generations. Thanks to Giulio I was introduced to the community of young designers. We would work until late in the day, often until night, and since his Venetian designer friend was fast asleep in the mezzanine of his studio, we used hold whispered conversations with each other. As I mentioned, things were hectic and I never managed to meet Luca. However I was struck by the close ties between the young designers who converged on Milan from all over Italy for the Salone, especially by the way they tried to help one another and work together, in a sense moving as a group. Networking like this was the only way they could carve out a space for themselves.

The critical euphoria was running particularly high in the days of the Salone, and this group of young designers (together with their mentor Beppe Finessi) developed their own ritual for celebrating its end by getting together around a big table where the discussions were lively. This last supper was the place where they subjected each new project to subtle analysis, thrashing out its details, weaknesses and strong points, discussing the heroes of the moment, the businesses and their experiences with them, swapping tips and helping one another. It was a community charged with intense energy, yet they felt they were being left on the margins of the dominant system, which seemed to be giving them neither attention nor space. They appeared more interested in forming ties with industry, which the Radical movement had always called into question, while they saw it as a privileged partner, choosing to act with it. This was a community of young people looking for their place in the sun.

This general scenario makes it easy to understand why Nichetto's decision to bypass Milan and gravitate elsewhere was strategic in his career, taking him to Stockholm in 2011 while keeping an office in Italy. His career developed internationally in the very years when such an expansion of scale was felt more than ever to be necessary, in an economy that was becoming increasingly interconnected and disrupted by the prospect of a single large market.

Francesca Picchi is an architect, journalist and independent curator, who lives in Milan. For sixteen years she was on the editorial staff of *Domus* magazine. Exhibitions she has curated include *Enzo Mari. Il lavoro al centro* (Santa Monica Art Centre, Barcelona, 1999 and Triennale Milano, 2000), *Kuramata's Tokyo* (Zegna Space, Milan, 2003) and *The Business of People* (14th International Architecture Exhibition, Venice Biennale, 2014). She teaches Design History at ISIA in Florence.

NICHETTO STUDIO PROJECTS

001. Salviati, Millebolle, 2000

The Millebolle vase – meaning 'a thousand bubbles' – is created using the refined techniques of Venetian master glassblowers. Large air bubbles are embedded in the surface by a master glazier in a difficult, experimental process that requires unceasing concentration. Each piece is unique, and the bubbles form an elegant decoration that catches the light. →

002. Salviati, Bubble, 2002

This work is blown by hand using an ancient Venetian glass technique, whereby layers of coloured and clear glass sheets are manipulated into a sinuous silhouette with its four spheres. Glass cuts on the top and sides reveal a bright green interior beneath the opaque red exterior. A limited-edition series of 101 pieces designed with Gianpietro Gai. →

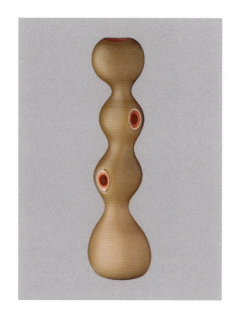

003. Foscarini, O-Space, 2003

Crafted from high-density expanded polyurethane, the O-Space light is shaped like a compressed letter O, with a small bulb at its bottom that shines both directly down into the room and up into the void at the centre of the O, reflecting light around the room. Designed with Gianpietro Gai. →

004. Salviati, Spoon, 2004

Each piece in this family of decorative objects serves two distinct functions. Placed vertically, they are vases; placed horizontally, they work as bowls. Spoon vases are suited to displaying a variety of items. Crafted from glass with a glossy, coloured sheen, they are named after the piece of cutlery that they resemble. →

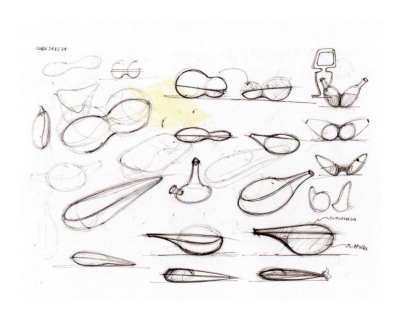

006. Kristalia, Face, 2005

Face's minimal aesthetics help it to harmonize with a variety of items in both domestic and public spaces. Combining functionality with comfort, Face's lightweight form allows it to be conveniently stacked, while the space in its backrest encourages the natural flexibility of the user's back and makes the chair easier to carry. →

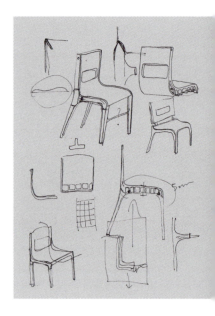

007. Bosa Ceramiche, Umbravase, 2007

A vase that also functions as an umbrella stand. Its two vessels allow it to conveniently hold numerous small and large umbrellas, which can be easily withdrawn and replaced. Cast in ceramic, Umbravase has an organic form and earthy colouration that evoke objects from the natural world, and suit a variety of contexts. Umbravase can even be used as a distinctive pot for large plants. →

005. Bosa Ceramiche, Hook Box, 2005

Created as an efficient solution to a common problem, the Hook Box is a multipurpose storage unit. Its compact form includes a box for holding small items and a lip on which clothes can be hung. The Hook Box thereby lets a user hang a coat and store important, easily misplaced objects – such as keys – in the same place. →

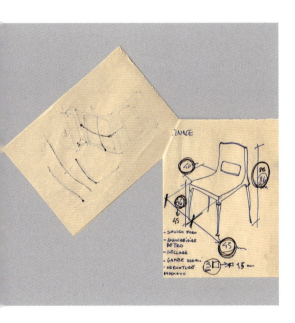

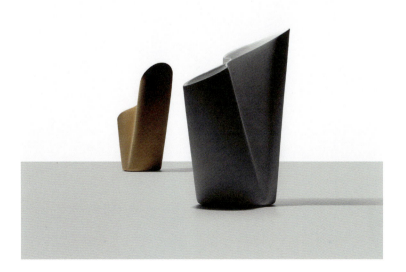

008. Kristalia, Dart, 2007

A bar stool in colourful polypropylene with an elegant S-curve design. A discrete seating pad guarantees comfort, while the lightweight aluminium swivel base and adjustable height let it adapt to a variety of different environments. As such, the stool works just as well at the kitchen counter as it does around an office meeting table. →

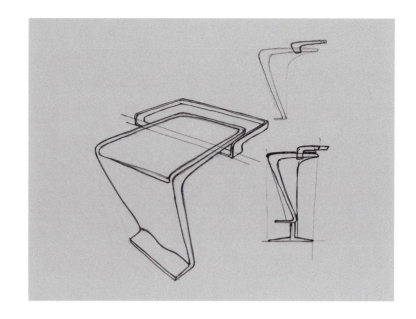

009. Italesse, Stripe, 2008

This dining tray made from ABS plastic features a black outer band structure that wraps around a coloured, soft-touch, anti-slip plate. Stripe's sleek, sinuous profile carries a sense of futurism. The high inner walls make serving safe in all situations, while its firmness allows dishes and glasses to be transported easily. Stripe combines a powerful aesthetic with complete functionality. →

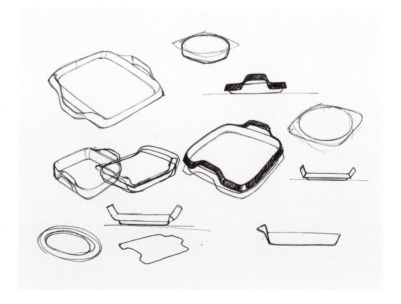

DEFINING A NEW ITALIAN DESIGN LANGUAGE

EERO KOIVISTO IN CONVERSATION WITH MAX FRASER

Defining a new Italian Design Language.
Eero Koivisto in conversation with Max Fraser

Max Fraser: Are you able to cast your mind back to how you and Luca first met?

Eero Koivisto: I have a faint memory that it was in Stockholm during the furniture fair, but I don't recall the year – it was a long time ago now! We had a coffee and started talking but I remember that his English was dreadful, it was really, really bad. He won't mind me saying this because, of course, now his English is really good!

MF: Luca would describe you rather like an older brother to him. He told me you were very encouraging when he first moved to Sweden.

EK: Luca's wife, Åsa, decided that she wanted to go back to Sweden to live. Luca reluctantly moved too. I remember we had dinner at a temporary apartment they were living in. It was winter so it was cold and dark. After dinner, Luca and I went out on to the balcony and he was anxious about the move, believing that his whole career would go down the drain by moving to Sweden because all of his contacts were in Italy. I had to reassure him, so I said the move was going to be good for him because people would treat him as exotic; in Sweden he would be the exotic Italian and in Italy he would be the exotic Italian who moved to Sweden. And look what happened!

Somebody told me once that if you go to Milan, it's like being in a big cage of yellow birds. Even if we are based in Stockholm and one of the bigger blue birds, when we go to Milan, we will always be a little exotic blue bird among all the yellow birds. I think Luca is an exotic yellow bird here in Stockholm and an exotic blue bird in Milan!

MF: How would you describe Luca's design language?

EK: I think he's very Mediterranean in his design language. When he moved to Stockholm, he had his eyes wide open to Swedish design and was looking at others much more then – he's a naturally curious guy. I think if you look at his design language over the last three to five years, it's grown to be more Italian in my opinion, more extrovert in a way.

MF: You mean he's expressing the Italian in him a bit more?

EK: Well, in some ways, I think him moving here has made him more Italian! That's just my theory. For many designers, it takes time to establish your design language; I think the move to Sweden made him find his.

I've worked on various design projects with him and he often refers to Italy and Venice when he's sketching new ideas and in his conversation, telling stories about the way they do things in Venice … so I think the Italian in him has surfaced and become much stronger now that he is out of Italy.

In one way Luca is renewing Italian design because, of course, he is very influenced by his Venetian heritage, but then he adds influences from different places in the world, puts it all into his mixer and out comes something that is his own! I think there should be a big exhibition about him in Venice one day.

MF: How is Luca's style different from that of his established Italian predecessors?

EK: When I refer to Italian design, I'm thinking about the sort of very elegant style that has been around since the 1960s, produced by companies like Minotti, B&B Italia and Living Divani. They all have this very polished and timeless style. But I think Luca's style is much wilder somehow. It's moving fast in a way. You know, he used to play basketball, and in his design work I think he is moving like a basketball player, bouncing from one part of the field to the other. It's really interesting to find somebody who is working in this kind of different Italian language.

MF: How do you think a product needs to communicate in an age of so much showmanship?

EK: Everything is image-driven today. If you look at design right at this very moment, there are many design cultures moving at the same time. Furniture right now is extrovert in its language. If you look back only twenty years [to 2000], minimalist designers did minimalist stuff and maximalists did maximalist stuff, but now it's all mixed up and I think that's really good.

MF: What have you learned from the way Luca operates?

EK: I learned a sort of seriousness from him about our profession. As well as Luca's laughter, good mood and jokes, business-wise he knows exactly what he's doing at every moment.

MF: Luca likes to remain a sort of outsider. For example, if he feels like he's getting too close to the Stockholm design scene, he pushes back against it. Have you noticed that?

EK: I feel the same way; maybe that's why we like each other! I think it's smart not to be too associated with any scene at all. The moment you are popular, the only thing you know is that you will be unpopular!

MF: What is your diagnosis of the design scene at the moment?

EK: Do you want a positive or a negative answer?! Well, I've been working for about thirty years now [since about 1990]. I'm really happy that people want the kind of work we do and we can survive on it. But I think the importance of design will never be what it was around the millennium because I don't believe the next generation of young people are so interested in material things any more – there are other things that are more important to them now. A larger chunk of society doesn't really care about design, they just take it for granted somehow.

On the positive side, I think that as more products become non-existent, it becomes even more important that the few that are left should be designed well. And that is where we fit in.

MF: Yes, when it feels as though we're just tweaking iterations of the same thing, inevitably that question 'Do we need more chairs?' comes up. But design's capabilities in terms of tackling problems in other areas of society are quite untapped and there's huge potential in those areas.

EK: Yes, but most people are not interested in it, that's the truth. Also, there are huge double standards going on in the whole design industry as it is right now. There's so much greenwashing out there, it really makes me angry.

I would gladly work on some of these problems if somebody asked me to, but it's very difficult to get anybody to pay for it. So, we do it the other way around and try to push a more sustainable path with the people we work with. At least it feels like we're doing something positive in that regard.

I believe that objects should be manufactured in an ethical way by skilled people. They should be made to a good quality so that they will last a long time. That's the best you can do. The best chair you can make is a chair that will never be recycled. Somebody will use it throughout their life and then pass it on and then somebody else will buy it second-hand and use it … that's good design. If it's made to a good standard by people who can make a living out of it and sustain a decent life … that's good manufacturing too.

MF: What do you think Luca's lasting contribution to the field of design might be?

EK: It's interesting to think about the ways in which he is moving other people. Luca has shown young Italians that you can move somewhere else, and make it work. I suspect a lot of young Italians are looking up to him because he has shown that it is possible to go out into the world and make a mark.

MF: What does it take to make a success of yourself in the design business?

EK: Well, it's a really tough profession and you have to be very consistent and strong-minded, and you have to be passionate. Regardless of their style, I would say that the designers who make it in the end are the ones who are very passionate and very skilled at what they do.

There are many people who want to be designers but there is very little work to go around. The designers who are left are passionate. I think Luca clearly has that passion, strong will – and talent of course!

Eero Koivisto is one third of Claesson Koivisto Rune, the architecture and design studio established with Mårten Claesson and Ola Rune in Stockholm in 1995. As well as having a stronghold in Sweden, the multidisciplinary nature of their work takes the trio across the world, completing entire hotel schemes as well as designing all the items you would expect to find throughout the interior. The products they create, including furniture, lighting and accessories, are manufactured by some of the finest brands in the business, including Arflex, Cappellini, Fontana Arte, Offecct and Wästberg, and have attracted awards and plaudits internationally. When Luca Nichetto moved to Stockholm from Venice in 2011, Koivisto helped him to find his feet and they developed a strong friendship.

010. Italesse, Titan, 2008

A thermal carafe, available in a range of colours. An external APS structure encloses a removable, insulating inner polypropylene flask. Titan is equipped with a flow-adjustment button for ice shut-off, and a silicone safety strap. Several units can be stacked for convenient storage, and Titan can be easily carried for serving. →

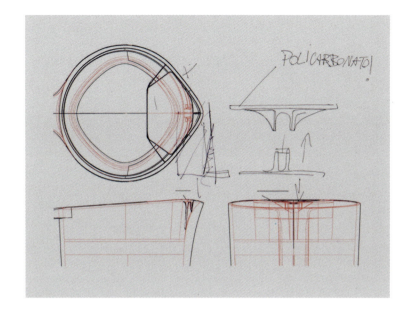

011. Casamania, Stereo, 2008

Stereo is a complete seating system, produced with wooden legs or as a stackable chair with thin metal legs. An open, versatile design with multiple possibilities for use in different contexts, Stereo is available in a wide range of colours, material and functions. The polyproplylene seat is glossy in the rear and opaque in front, and can be either partially or completely upholstered. →

012. Kristalia, Plate 46/50, 2008

With its striking lines and streamlined forms, the Plate family of office chairs is designed to evoke the speed and sleekness of racing cars. Plate's slender legs give a sense of lightness, and are complemented by an upholstered seat for enhanced comfort. Plate 46/50 – the smallest chair in the series – can fit into a variety of spaces and is available with or without armrests. →

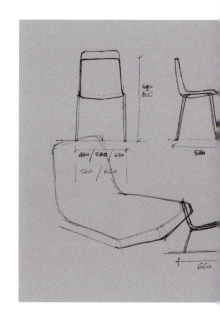

015. Italesse, Icesac, 2009

Electronic ice-crushers are needlessly power-intensive; Icesac offers a different option. Made from soft, resistant silicone, it lets the user crush ice manually. After the ice cubes are inserted, and the crusher tied together with a ribbon to prevent spillage, the crusher can be smashed on a counter or with a pestle to create the perfect cocktail ice. With its bold, durable design, Icesac can also be filled with water and stood up to make a striking vase for flowers. →

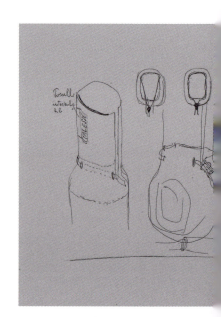

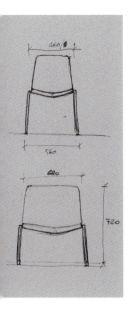

013. Bosa Ceramiche, Essence Collection, 2009

Essence is a set of eight ceramic objects inspired by the tools and techniques used by traditional Venetian craftsmen. It was created in collaboration with the ceramic company Bosa and glass manufacturer Venini, bringing together a team of local talent. After being exhibited in Venice by the architectural practice Laboratorio 2729, Essence travelled to Paris's 107 rue de Rivoli and London's Vessel Gallery, promoting the skilful handiwork of classic Italian artisans. →

014. Casamania, Nuance, 2009

Too many products waste high-quality fabric, disposing of offcuts rather than applying them for a new purpose. The Nuance chair and ottoman remedy this problem by using material that would otherwise be discarded. The chair's wide foam structure is spacious and comfortable, while its use of small fabric creates a striking display in a range of shades. Built with care, in the style of master artisans, Nuance manages to be both high-quality and environmentally conscious. →

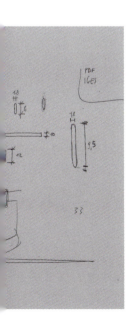

016. Nodus by Il Piccolo, Geoart, 2009

Geoart is a set of six small carpet modules, all handwoven from wool and silk. Each module is irregularly shaped, and can be combined with the others to create an overlapping effect to the owner's specifications. Inspired by Asia's diverse carpet-making traditions, and the materials, patterns and methods involved in those traditions, each Geoart module is produced in a different country and evokes a different tradition, spanning from China to Turkey. →

017. Foscarini, Troag, 2010

On a visit to Lapland, Luca Nichetto discovered the *tråg*, a canoe-shaped bowl used for crushing fruit and rising bread. Inspired by its form, he created his own boat-shaped Troag in the form of a suspension lamp. Rather than a traditional fabric lampshade, Troag is made from a single piece of curved wood. Slits in the wood allow the light to travel up and down, creating an intense effect that is suited to illuminating both long tables and large open spaces. →

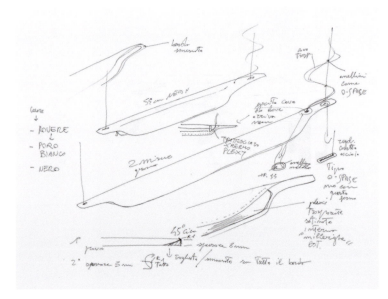

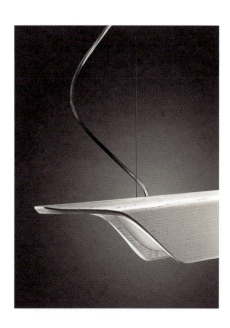

PROJECT 137
STEINWAY & SONS
GRAN NICHETTO

Project 137: Steinway & Sons, Gran Nichetto

New York feels like home. I have a family of friends and colleagues there whom I tend to visit at least once a year. In May 2018 I was travelling to the city, as I always do around that time of year, to attend the local Design Week, and especially to visit my friends Marc Thorpe, a super-talented designer and architect, and his wife, Claire Pijoulat, co-founder of WantedDesign.

Like a typical tourist landing in the city, I usually post a picture on my social media portraying Manhattan's skyline captioned with the phrase 'Good Morning NY'. It's my guilty pleasure since I'm not really a social-media addict, although these platforms have increasingly played a pivotal role in forging connections across the industry. That's what happened that May – social media led me to a most unexpected collaboration.

Jet-lagged and tired, I was catching up with Marc in Dumbo when I received a LinkedIn message from none other than Robert Polan, who headed the limited-edition piano department at Steinway & Sons. I was flabbergasted; there seemed to be a chance emerging for me to follow in the footsteps of the likes of Karl Lagerfeld, Damien Hirst and Lenny Kravitz, to name just a few.

When Steinway & Sons came knocking at the door, I knew I wanted my design approach to be as respectful to the object as it could be, since I could not even play the piano. I'd rather give the external structure a makeover, leaving the internal part as it is, as one would do when working on a car design. Visiting the legendary piano-maker's facility in Long Island felt like a trip to Willy Wonka's chocolate factory, and my excitement only grew stronger – the level of craftsmanship was astounding.

Our relationship was built on a very friendly and relaxed dynamic, despite the number of technical hurdles that had to be crossed before my limited-edition piano design eventually came to life. It required the same level of complexity as designing an entire building. As much as craftsmanship and artisanal know-how are embedded in the company's DNA, partnerships can result in fruitful learning curves for both parties. By his own admission, Robert is a 'product guy', and among my goals I was committed to bringing design practice and culture into the company.

After that seminal project, since 2019 I've had the unofficial role of creative director for limited-edition and custom pianos at Steinway & Sons, helping the company link with other designers and connect with speciality suppliers. My designer's ego was undoubtedly satisfied by working with such an institution, but the friendships I built at the company, starting with Robert, remain not only a great 'side effect' but also the engine by which my work with them thrives.

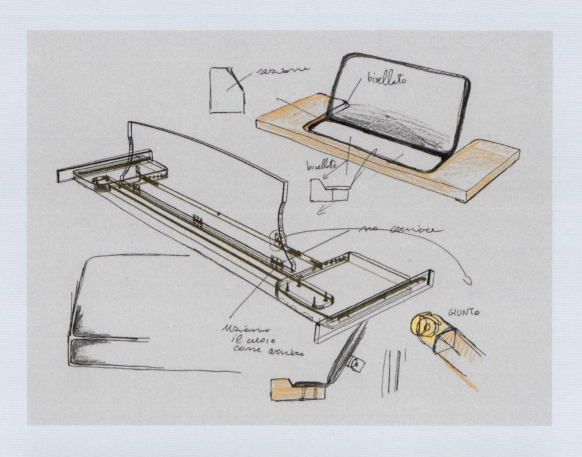

30.

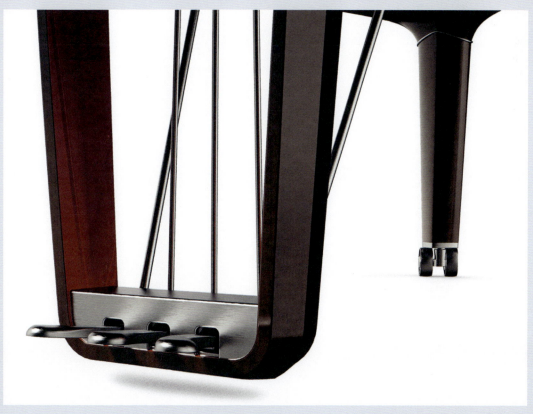

Type: Musical Instrument
Material: Wood, Metal, Leather
Colour: Various
Team: Massimo Minchio
Time: 2022
Producer: Steinway & Sons

018. Italesse, Bcool, 2010

In hot weather, it can be difficult to keep drinks cool. The Bcool drinks cooler makes the process simple. Shaped to hold conventionally sized beer and wine bottles, Bcool's sleek outer form belies its ribbed interior. By ensuring that drinks do not touch the external walls, these ribs allow the cooler's contents to remain chilled for longer. Inspired by the internal mechanisms that prevent computers from overheating, Bcool offers a simple solution to a common problem. →

019. Italesse, Venti4 Set, 2010

In traditional Italian cooking, dinner is preceded by a selection of antipasti. The Venti4 Set is designed for the easy serving of such meals. It centres on a large plate, with two cross-shaped, four-section dishes that can be stacked atop the plate to contain sauces and side dishes. A range of bowls, four small and one medium-sized, completes the set. Versatile enough to adapt to every need, Venti4 facilitates a wide range of serving practices in both professional and domestic contexts. →

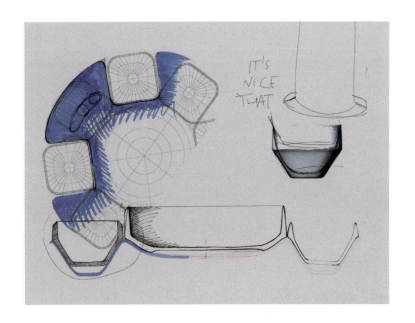

021. Venini, Arillo, 2010

Located just north of Venice, the islands of Murano are world-renowned for their glassmaking. Arillo is a collection of opaline vases that draw on this rich history. Crafted by master glassblowers using traditional techniques, the vases, like Venice itself, are influenced by both East and West: their light-catching vertical stripes evoke the shimmering patterns of Venetian beads, while their rounded form echoes the iconic shape of the Chinese lantern. →

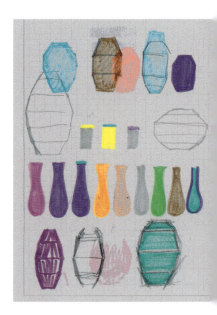

022. Venini, Otto, 2010

To become a master glassmaker, one must learn to blow glass with grace and fluidity, creating objects that appear pure and seamless. The Otto collection redefines the archetypical cylindrical glass vase as an elegantly curved form. Modelled on the number 8 (hence the collection's name), the rim is left open to reveal multicoloured layers that shift in the light. →

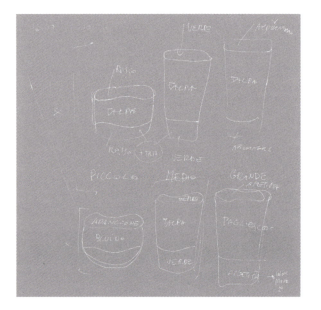

020. Offecct, Robo, 2010

In Chris Cunningham's video for Björk's 'All Is Full of Love' (1999), a pair of robots appear to gain emotional consciousness, ultimately kissing and embracing. Inspired by this film, the Robo chair has a sleek, futuristic aesthetic, and its forward-looking form is reflected in the environmentally friendly materials used in its construction. As with Meccano toys, which are constructed and dismantled by the user, the Robo's separate components can be disassembled and placed in a compact box, allowing easy, efficient transport. (See page 217.)

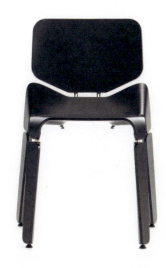

023. Fornasarig, Wolfgang Collection, 2011

In 2011 Luca Nichetto extended his practice outside Italy, taking up residence with Stockholm's Studio Wolfgang. To celebrate this new collaborative chapter in his practice, Nichetto designed the Wolfgang family of chairs, which are inspired by the material-sensitive work of the furniture-makers Hans J. Wegner and Michael Thonet. →

THE GREAT MATCHMAKER
ROBERT POLAN IN CONVERSATION WITH MAX FRASER

The Great Matchmaker.
Robert Polan in conversation with Max Fraser

Max Fraser: How did you first cross paths with Luca?

Robert Polan: I had been leading this effort to try and focus on our design strategy at Steinway & Sons. I don't come from a design background; I'm a product guy but I'm not a design guy. It's been a discovery for me to learn about the design world and about how design is purposefully done.

Part of my research and education was just meeting people in the craft. I started networking through some of the designers that I had been introduced to, and Luca's name kept coming up. During Design Week in New York in 2017, I saw that he was speaking at the event. I sent him a note via LinkedIn and he replied quickly; there was no pomp, he just said, 'Sure, would you like to get a coffee?' Shortly afterwards we met, had a coffee and hit it off. I invited him for a tour of the factory the next day and the relationship started from there; a very informal, unpretentious connection.

MF: What was your original proposition to Luca?

RP: Every few years, we create a series of limited-edition pianos. It's a way of creating something unique for Steinway & Sons and it certainly challenges us. At the time, I was trying to find the right designers to work with for that purpose. My initial thought was, could he be one of those designers?

MF: What is the history of Steinway & Sons's limited-edition pianos?

RP: Within Steinway & Sons, we use the term 'art cases' as a loose term to describe anything that's not a standard piano because it's been painted by someone or is customized or bespoke in some way. In the early days, the first head of the art-case department was a member of the Tiffany family, Joseph Burr Tiffany, and he worked with different artists and craftspeople customizing and drawing special designs for clients.

That work has ebbed and flowed throughout the history of Steinway & Sons. A lot of the work in the 80s and early 90s was with the designers who were furniture builders for the American studio craft world, such as Wendell Castle. Steinway & Sons worked with a lot of the great furniture makers in the US. We've also collaborated with great international designers like Karl Lagerfeld; he did a beautiful design that I believe is one of the more innovative ones that we've done in our history.

So, there's been this thread of design collaborations, but it slowed down in recent years. There wasn't necessarily a concerted effort to think about creating these custom pianos and having a bespoke division of Steinway & Sons until I joined. I've been helping create focus for Steinway & Sons to establish more of a design direction that has the ability to respond to custom and bespoke requests, and also collaborate with great designers who have the creative vision of today. And that's how I got involved with Steinway & Sons in 2016, and how I'm now working with Luca.

MF: Steinway & Sons's archives must be rich and varied. Do you access them often?

RP: Oh yes! One of the amazing parts of working for a company with history like Steinway & Sons is that we have so many records and files that date back to the beginning and we're fortunate to have maintained them. I can go back to the records room and pull from many file cabinets containing the original folders that date back to the late nineteenth century. We have what we call 'sketch files' holding all the different designs one after another. There are hundreds of them with all the original blueprints, samples, documentation and correspondence between suppliers of the day. You'll find fabric swatches and handwritten letters from different employees to the suppliers they worked with, and sometimes the original bill of sale to the customer. It's this great record of history that's not digitized, it's all in its original analogue form.

As a product person, when I started looking through those files, it was like walking into the archives of the British Museum or the Metropolitan Museum of Art. It's like being a kid every time I walk into that room; it's my candy shop!

MF: I would assume that musical instruments are designed by specialist instrument designers and not necessarily furniture designers. Which elements of the piano could an external designer change?

RP: The internal part of the piano, which is often called the 'harp', is a cast-iron plate with the soundboard and strings. That can't be changed because that's what has evolved into the Steinway

& Sons sound that makes us famous. However, the exterior of the piano can be customized around the internal functioning parts – what we call the 'case' or 'cabinet' and certain other visual and functional components. As long as you're not blocking the sound projection, there's a lot that can be done to customize a piano, and that is what we ask external designers to work on.

MF: What is it that attracted you to Luca's work?

RP: When I look at his work, there's a really interesting balance of art and sculpture; his experience in glassmaking really shows through; there's a lot of colour; forms are organic; it doesn't feel difficult to relate to and I'm visually attracted to it. But I think what really solidified that was the person, not just the design. For me, what works so well with Luca is him. It's his personality.

I like to joke that if he didn't have this success in design, he would make a great matchmaker. He's so good at connecting people and helping them find what they need through his network. His craft fits well with what we do, and that's ultimately what makes it so much fun to work with him.

MF: How would you describe the working dynamic between you and Luca?

RP: It's very friendly working environment. I think of Luca as a friend as much as I do a colleague. He has really invested a tremendous amount of personal energy into helping us, introducing us to other designers and his peers.

For his piano design, he designed a very complicated project, one that had difficult technical challenges, and so he worked very closely with our engineers to take his design and translate it into something that could be manufacturable.

When it gets into the experience of building a piano, we have to make certain choices, and he's great at helping us figure out how to keep the design intact without compromising either the design integrity or the piano's needs. He's great at sketching and thinking through solutions. He's extremely well connected, even just with suppliers, finding the right textile, finding the right metal finisher. It's a real collaboration.

MF: And now Luca has taken on the unofficial role of a creative director. How did that evolve?

RP: I probably knew when we first started to talk that he had the potential to be a creative director, but I wasn't quite sure we wanted one. But when I first visited him in Venice and spent time in his studio, I could see his process for sketching the design, the way he spoke about his understanding of manufacturing, and it all felt like this was the guy we needed to help us make things more purposeful and strategic. It's not an official title, but I would say it's functionally what he does for us today.

MF: What have you personally learned from working with Luca?

RP: I've learned so much. I think I've got a better understanding of how to view design and how to appreciate it. I think I was very quick to reject new ideas, and Luca has helped me really understand how to absorb new concepts and feel comfortable moving beyond what might be a traditional or a current design language. It's been helpful to train my mind to be more open to new ideas.

Also, I think he's very clear in his design vision and knows what he wants and that it can be done, and I think it's been helpful for our team. We have the confidence that we can build exactly what the designer imagines; we know we can accomplish that and Luca's very helpful in staying focused on achieving it.

MF: Do you have any funny anecdotes from your time with Luca?

RP: Well, more of a coincidence; we were born in the same month of the same year, so there's a chemistry that just works. We are both equally stubborn. Luca knows what he wants, and he's comfortable asking for it. He's a great collaborator!

Robert Polan lives in New York and has worked as the Vice President of Custom Pianos at Steinway & Sons since 2016, joining the team within the historical domain of this world-famous piano manufacturer. The company, which was founded in Germany in 1853 before moving to Queens, New York, in 1880, can boast a rich heritage as well as serial innovations in the piano world. The company is recognized not only by the most renowned musicians but also by the individuals and families who want to own the best piano they can find.

024. Globo, Affetto Collection, 2011

Characterized by its kinetic energy and welcoming contours, Affetto is a line of bathroom fixtures and accessories that are at home in any type of interior. Affetto was inspired by the Modernist design of the 1950s, and its simple, elegant forms create a strong, sculptural aesthetic. →

025. Offecct, Greenpads, 2011

Designed for Offecct as part of its Oasis initiative, Greenpads are stool-like stands for displaying potted plants. The stands consist of a single aluminium leg topped with several saucer-like trays. Inspired by the architecture of the 1960s, in which vegetation was often treated as an integral aspect of the design, Greenpads can be placed alone or in clusters, allowing the user to create large patches of greenery that enhance the aesthetic and air quality of their environment. →

026. Prosciutteria King's, Design House, 2011

Prosciutto is one of Italy's greatest culinary exports. Nichetto was asked to design a stylish yet functional set of ham-carving instruments for Prosciutteria King's, creating a new brand identity for the company. These products were exhibited at Milan Design Week, in an exhibition space that featured ham-carving demonstrations and sampling. The area was decorated with Nichetto's furniture and lighting for a range of the world's leading brands, evoking the luxury of old Venetian salons. →

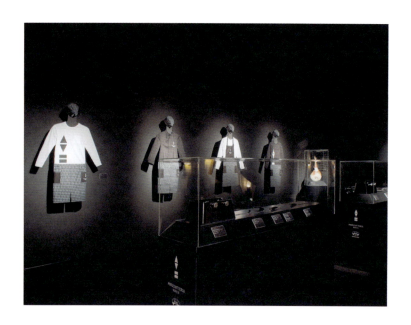

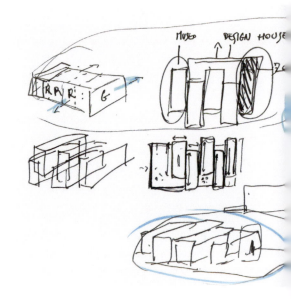

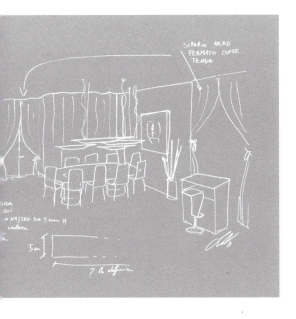

027. Prosciutteria King's, Knives, 2011

Charged with creating a strong brand identity for the charcutier Prosciutteria King's, Luca Nichetto designed a complete set of tools that encompasses every aspect of the prosciutto-carving process: knives, tongs and holder. The ham and boning knives have a steel blade, on which is imprinted King's sleek new logo. In the premium version, presented in a wooden case, the blade has a black coating, making it stand out as a stylish and professional kitchen tool. →

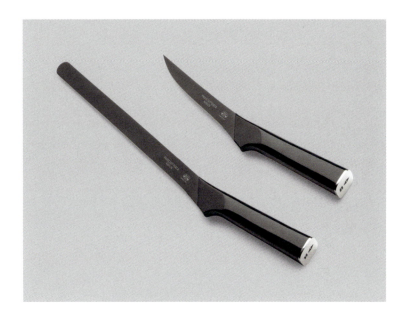

028. Foscarini, Plass, 2011

The Plass lampshade reinterprets the Murano glassblowing tradition in the light of new processes and materials. Named as a fusion of glass and plastic, Plass is created by rotation-moulding transparent polycarbonate. The resulting object features the transparency of handmade glass and its natural irregularities, accentuated by the light bulb within. (See page 199.)

029. Cassina, Torei, 2012

Named after the Japanese term for a tray, the Torei family of tables is inspired by the compactness and flexibility of serving trays. Elegant metal legs support an ash-wood or Carrara marble top, with folded edges that convey refinement. Torei's various configurations grant it true versatility, letting it work independently, in tandem with a sofa, or arranged alongside other products in the family to create a striking assemblage of display tables. →

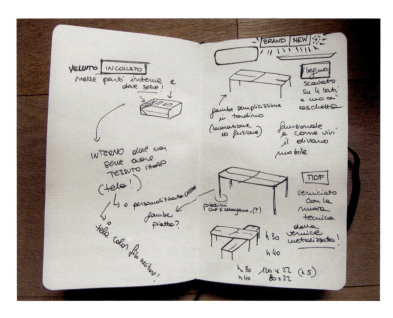

030. Established & Sons, Golconda, 2012

The Golconda lamp is named after the painting of 1953 by René Magritte in which dozens of businessmen in black suits and bowler hats fall from the sky like raindrops. With its spun aluminium shade – which resembles the hats in the painting – appearing to float above an off-centre conical base, the Golconda draws on the kind of surrealism that Magritte specialized in. The asymmetrical pairing of base and shade allows the lamp to rotate and cast light beyond its own centre of gravity, illuminating a large swathe of the surface below. →

PROJECT 133
GINORI 1735
LCDC COLLECTION

Project 133: Ginori 1735, LCDC Collection

There's often a thread linking diverse and faraway fields and industries. This was the case with my project for Ginori 1735, unveiled in September 2021 at Milan Design Week, in which product design, perfume-making, cinematic storytelling and Catherine de' Medici all played a role.

The same can be said for my professional relationships, when people I've met years earlier sometimes return front and centre in my career later on. As a case in point, I had met Annalisa Tani, brand and product manager at Ginori 1735, when she worked at the textile specialist Zucchi, and asked her to collaborate on a project I was doing for the Portuguese-British furniture company De La Espada, which was exhibited in Paris at the Maison&Objet trade fair in 2015.

Fast-forward to 2019 and Annalisa had me train my design skills on a project for Ginori 1735, the homeware and porcelain brand, having appreciated my work ever since our encounter in 2015. She was particularly impressed by a fragrance flacon I had worked on in collaboration with A. W. Bauer & Co., the most storied tailoring company in Scandinavia, and my friend Ben Gorham, founder of the perfume house Byredo.

Working with heritage companies with such a strong legacy as Ginori 1735 always makes a difference. This time I was also pushing myself as a designer to explore a lifestyle- rather than design-orientated approach. The first time I visited Ginori's archives in Florence, accompanied by Alessandro Badii, one of the brand's team (which also includes Rebecca Rizzello, Marta Bellina, Debora De Faveri, Letizia Baglioni, Lucia Mastroiacovo and the company's CEO, Alain Prost), I was mesmerized and had the unique opportunity to scrutinize at first hand its rich history and transition from a decorative homeware and porcelain company to the hotbed of Italian design spearheaded in the 1920s by Gio Ponti.

My brief was to develop a collection of home-fragrance holders, and back in my Stockholm studio I started obsessing over the link between Florence and the art of perfume-making. The city had gained quite a reputation after the Dominican friars there started producing fragrances using plants and flowers from the Tuscan countryside. Incidentally, Venice, my home town, had a similar history, which made the project all the more exciting.

When Catherine de' Medici moved to the French court to marry Henri d'Orléans in 1533, her entourage went with her, including Renato Bianco, her master perfumier. For my collection, I envisioned a present-day trip, associating each home-fragrance object in the collection with a particular character – the lover, the Amazon, the prophet, the scholar – and weaving a story around them.

Far from orchestrating this project as a nostalgic look at Catherine's heyday, my design journey landed me on references as diverse as the films of Sofia Coppola's and Baz Luhrmann, as well as the designer and director Jean-Paul Goude's outrageous aesthetic.

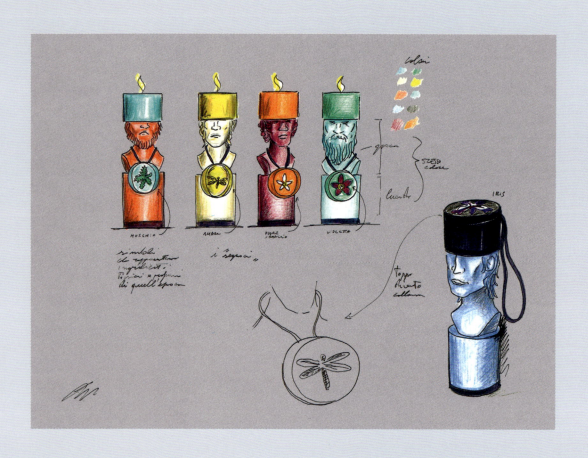

Type: Home Fragrance
Material: Porcelain, Glass, Perfumed Wax
Colour: Various
Team: Luca Nichetto
Time: 2021
Client: Ginori 1735

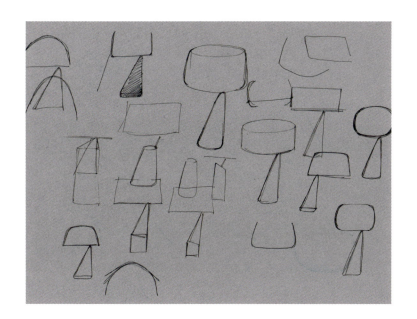

031. Foscarini, Stewie, 2012

Named after the famous *Family Guy* character, the Stewie floor lamp's distinctive design resembles a vintage television. It was inspired by an unusually located washbasin in Luca Nichetto's Venice studio, which offered the challenge of creating a new type of light from unconventional materials. Stewie's light source is hidden behind textiles, providing a different sort of illumination from that of conventional lamps. The lamp can be turned towards a wall to create a softer glow. →

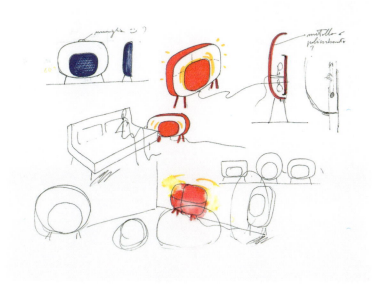

032. Gallery Pascale, Les Poupées, 2012

This is a single object that combines two functions: vase and candle-holder. Composed of a larger ceramic torso and a small blown-glass head, Les Poupées – which is named after the French word for 'dolls' – resembles an abstracted form of a human body. It is inspired by the pure aesthetic of the Finnish glassmaker Timo Sarpaneva, the bold colours of the Italian architect Ettore Sottsass and Japanese *kokeshi* wooden dolls, which famously lack arms and legs. →

033. Cassina, La Mise, 2012

La Mise is a family of sofas inspired by the way a kimono wraps around its wearer. With a focus on comfort, each piece features a single piece of high-quality fabric that folds around the metal framework like a tailor-made dress. Natural folds form each time La Mise is used, granting it an empathetic quality that reacts to and reflects its users. (See page 181.)

034. La Chance, Float, 2012

Composed of an aluminium spun flat base and top in the shape of an inverted cone, Float gives the sense of floating on water, an impression that is compounded by the mirrored surface of the base. This sculptural aesthetic makes it a feature in any living area. Float's gravity-defining form was created using metal-turning technology that is usually employed in aircraft manufacture. →

035. Cassina, Motek, 2013

In the traditional Japanese art of origami, paper is folded again and again until it becomes a work of art. With each fold, the delicate material strengthens. Designed for Cassina, Motek is a lightweight chair inspired by the firmness of origami. All models feature a pressure-moulded felt shell that allows the fabric to bear the user's weight while remaining comfortable and soft. The backrest and sides of the seat feature graceful folds for extra support. →

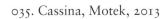
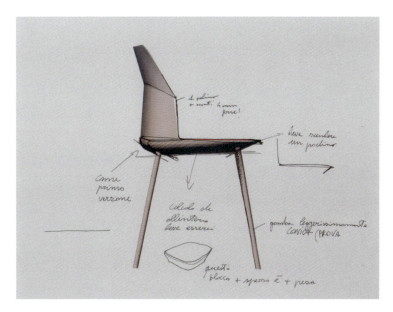

036. IMM Cologne, Das Haus, 2013

For the 2013 edition of IMM Cologne's Das Haus series, Luca Nichetto created *Interiors on Stage*, an installation that placed greenery at the centre of architecture. Plants were carefully matched to each domestic situation, from aromatic spice plants in the kitchen to purifying plants in the bathroom. Inspired by Californian Modernism, Japanese architecture and the work of the Italian architect Carlo Scarpa, Das Haus involved a colour palette of different pastels for each room and had an airy and open construction, with sight lines across the entire structure. →

PORCELAIN NEVER FORGETS

ALESSANDRO BADII IN CONVERSATION WITH FRANCESCA PICCHI

Porcelain Never Forgets.
Alessandro Badii in conversation with
Francesca Picchi

Francesca Picchi: The Ginori 1735 manufactory is one of the oldest in Europe and one of the most important in the production of artistic porcelain. Its proximity to Florence and the fact that the year of foundation is in the company name, reveal both its history and its figurative heritage: today we can see it as a sort of cathedral of manual work. Could you help us to understand how it functions, starting with your work?

Alessandro Badii: I work in the Style Office of Ginori 1735, where I'm the design coordinator. My department deals with the creative part of developing both white and decorated ware. Basically, my job is to enable ideas to become products.

For those not familiar with the organization of work in a porcelain factory, it can be said there are two main subdivisions: white and decorated. By white, we mean the pure porcelain product, and its production process is generally straightforward. A plaster mould is developed and liquid porcelain, called slip, is poured into it, or else the porcelain paste is pressed or modelled into shape. The mould is then opened and the piece fired for the first time at 1,000°C; at this point it might be decided to apply the glaze, which adds gloss to the piece. Then it's fired for a second time, at 1,400°C. Whatever's being made, whether it's dishes, statuettes or candlesticks, the preliminaries are always the same.

Decorated ware, on the other hand, is less straightforward. It's a tangled skein! The colour is added from a series of palettes, which creates endless variation. To this is added the further complexity of the many techniques available, and their order can also be changed to create any number of possible inventions. These two different and complementary styles determine the division of the work in the factory.

Then, when we work with outside designers, as we did with Luca Nichetto, all our manufacturing skills are involved, including modelling and the technical quality office, which is in charge of refining the specifications for production. In a manufactory, more than ever, the work has to be teamwork.

FP: What training did you have?

AB: My great good fortune was to learn the trade from the old masters, because it's not something I picked up at school. I was just finishing studying design at the Faculty of Architecture in Florence when I was taken on at Ginori 1735. Here I had the opportunity to work with one of the old factory masters, who specialized in developing decorated products. Alongside him, the master in charge of modelling, the master of the painters and the master of artistic slip-casting were seen rather romantically as the custodians of Ginori 1735's art. I spent the first six months doing watercolours on paper, outlines, drawings in Indian ink, various types of representation, and all these exercises improved my hand to a degree that I could never have imagined.

FP: What have you learned from working with a material like porcelain?

AB: Porcelain has an amazingly plastic quality that enables you to create extreme forms. It's a beautiful material but exceedingly delicate. You have to be immensely careful. If you make just a slightly more presumptuous gesture it will still show up in the material. Even opening a mould calls for the greatest care, because the slightest stress is enough to create a flaw that might appear only after firing. The masters said: 'Porcelain never forgets.' At first it looks fine, but it's only when the piece comes out of the kiln, after the final firing, that you discover that some flaw has crept into it. It's a living material. It warps, changes and always has an aura of mystery. It's like doing magic; you can't always explain things rationally. The challenge is invariably to make the pieces unique and fascinating, but at the same time each item has to come up to the standards of an industrial product.

FP: How did Luca's project fit into this set-up?

AB: When Luca presented the project and started telling his story, I was fascinated by the idea. I realized it was a perfect project, because it had storytelling and scope for development, it was perfectly feasible in porcelain and above all it had the magic that would enable it to make the most of Ginori 1735's experience.

The brief he was given was to design a line of fragrances, and he created his idea around the historical figure of the Florentine master perfumer who introduced the art of perfume to France. Luca imagined a story about the retinue of characters that Catherine de' Medici took with her to France when she married the Duke of Orléans, the future king of France. Among them was Renato Bianco, an alchemist trained in the art of preparing perfumes by the Dominican friars of Santa Maria Novella, who took him in as an orphan. He made the use of perfume widespread in France, where he was known as René le Florentin. It's a story that deserves to be better known, and it marked the start of the tradition of French perfume.

The court as Luca imagined it included a large collection of characters all engaged in the different functions associated with perfume. He imagined a series of very distinctive figures – the scholar, the lover, the favourite, the Amazon and many others – who appear as if in a procession heading for Paris. Re-creating this court in a material like porcelain called for very painstaking work on the human figure. And the figurative element gave us an opportunity for modelling in the finest tradition of the manufactory.

FP: Did you make use of the materials in Ginori 1735's historical archives?

AB: Luca's project drew on a deeply felt theme, which was to reinterpret the archive and the forms it contained in contemporary ways. The factory has an extraordinary collection of wax models, plaster casts and materials used by the workers. Over the years, Ginori 1735 has built up a historical archive of casts of famous statues in the history of art, so it was interesting to look for the right features in this great repertoire of human figures to give a face to each individual.

Ultimately, we worked on parts of the statues present in the archives by playing on the fact that they were not completely recognizable. This was bound up with the theme of magic and playfulness, and it was a way of adding a touch of irony, perhaps even impertinence, by featuring classical elements and touches from other periods, mingling styles to make the project even more fascinating.

Luca got quite carried away and drew a whole notebook full of these figures. To date we've only developed a few, but others are in the pipeline and I guess we'll eventually issue even more, so that in the coming years new characters will appear from his notebook. It's a work in progress.

Luca's project also enabled us to refresh our ideas about the rather neglected technique of coloured glazes, the glossy finish applied after the first firing. Colouring the glaze produces a wide range of hues with very different chiaroscuro values, even though everything is made from the same line of white porcelain, so optimizing production.

FP: The thing that has always struck me about porcelain manufactories is that the workers, the model makers and the painters, are all artists.

AB: There's healthy competition among Ginori 1735's staff, and perhaps this is one of the factors that enhances the company's drive. Working by hand in itself compels you to join forces with others and be a team player.

Absorbing external influences, supporting the work of a designer or artist while at the same time making it sustainable and developing it for serial production is the great challenge facing us every day. Porcelain has extraordinary potential. The fact that it's made possible by the creative involvement of such a large number of artists, as you rightly term them, makes it all the more extraordinary. It means giving a voice to a manufactory that is a giant that's been seated on the same spot for 300 years. It's an honour!

Part of the Kering Group since 2013, the Ginori 1735 manufactory is one of the oldest and most renowned European factories in artistic porcelain production. Alessandro Badii, Florentine by birth, joined Ginori 1735 in 2009 after studying at the Art Institute of Florence, and at the University of Florence. He is the design coordinator of the Ufficio Stile, the division created to deal with the creative side of product development. He also oversees the cooperation of various internal divisions, in particular when the company opens up to new collaborations, such as Luca Nichetto's collection.

037. Nodus by Il Piccolo, Regata Storica, 2013

Regata Storica is a hand-tufted rug made from fine Indian wool. It is inspired by Luca Nichetto's home town of Venice, where Eastern carpet-making techniques meet Western aesthetics. The name of this piece refers to an annual Venetian sporting event, a historical pageant and rowing race involving brightly painted vessels. Paying homage to this traditional event, the rug features a graphic depiction of these colourful boats, lined up as if ready to race. →

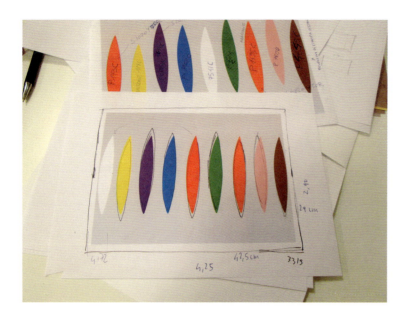

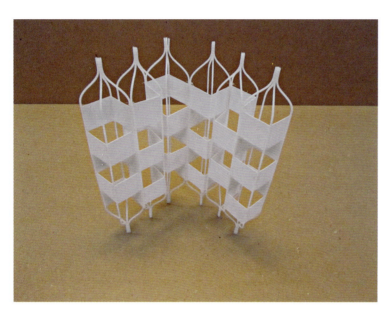

039. Offecct, Linea, 2013

In Osvaldo Cavandoli's popular cartoon 'La Linea', the protagonist both walks along and is part of an infinite line. Linea is a sofa inspired by this iconic character. Its back – blue, as in the animation – is decorated with intersecting grooves. These precisely shaped lines allow the possibility of creating a seamless succession of connected seats, linked by small side tables that provide additional functionality. →

040. Tales, Pavilion, 2013

The Tales Pavilion is a standalone furniture and product showroom in Beijing, and the first building to be completed by Nichetto Studio. The showroom's structure is concrete, while its facade is covered in 1,200 individual grass-like strands of brass that oxidize and change colour with the seasons. The architectural direction evokes the spirit of the young and avant-garde design distributor Tales, which commissioned the building. Much like grass, Tales is full of life and has a strong desire to grow. →

038. Nichetto = nendo, 2013

The *Nichetto = nendo* exhibition was a unique coming together of two designers connected by a collective vision. The exhibition, displayed at Milan Design Week in 2013, presented a collection of seven products that were created through a collaboration between Luca Nichetto and the Japanese designer Oki Sato, founder of nendo. Inspired by the Japanese tradition of *renga* poetry, in which one poet writes the first three lines and another the final two, Oki and Luca sent each other ideas to complete. The result was seven co-designed products and a lasting friendship. (See page 163.)

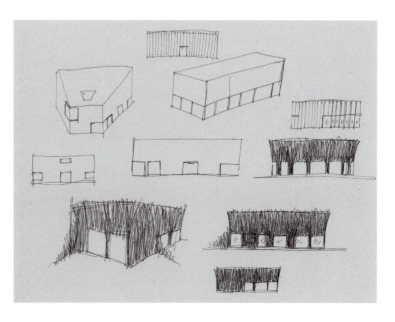

041. Arflex, Ladle, 2014

The Ladle family of armchairs casts a contemporary light on the style, feeling and comfort of classic armchairs of the 1960s. Although all the chairs have the same soft, spoon-like seat structure, each can be customized with three different backrests and the same number of legs. The chairs are available in wooden, tube metal or four-spoke swivel-and-tilt versions, and in small, medium and large variants, to suit spaces of all sizes. →

PROJECT 096
SANCAL
NEXT STOP

Project 096: Sancal, Next Stop

There are some projects that require more time to ripen than others. I first met the Danish textile designer Marie-Louise Rosholm ten years before we actually managed to realize an innovation that we had both envisioned, without being able to turn it into reality.

I had been dreaming of a sofa upholstery that would come out of the loom with no requirement for further hand-finishing or -stitching. When we first discussed my idea, I had sort of commissioned Marie-Louise, whom I had met thanks to our mutual friend, fashion designer Anthony Knight, to look out for suppliers and textile-makers who could help us on that front, but she had no luck until 2017.

That year, for the second time in the span of a couple of years, the Alicante-based furniture company Sancal came to me, this time tapping my studio for a full collection of four design pieces, including a sofa. Unexpectedly, Marie-Louise had also pursued her research into the fascinating textile world and had managed to find a proper solution, which entailed crafting the upholstery from a knitted textile made with the loom that would avoid any problem with the padding.

Sancal had briefed me to take my cue from Milan's Turati metro station, a great example of postmodernist architecture, and its geometric lines and colours of red, yellow and grey served as the main inspiration for each of the four pieces. For instance, the wooden and metal 'Next Stop' sofa referenced the symmetry of the train seats and the subway line M3's lighting to create an endless modular seating programme, in which the knitted textile was used as a joint between parts.

There was a sustainable silver lining to the project, too, in that the manufacturing process of the knitted fabric did not entail any leftovers, guaranteeing a zero-waste production process. Marie-Louise would call the upholstery Zero for this reason.

By proposing this innovative project to Sancal's team – spearheaded by the second generation of the founding family, sisters Esther and Elena Castaño-López, who brought a fresh insight to the company, growing it into a multidisciplinary atelier in its own right – we certainly pushed the storied Spanish brand to embrace out-of-the-box thinking and stand by an eco-friendly mission.

Furthermore, I acted as a bridge connecting different talents in the name of successful collaboration. By tapping me, Sancal got the benefit of Marie-Louise's unparalleled know-how, not to mention the textile supplier's exceptional craftsmanship. The project served as a launchpad for my studio to practise the art of connecting dots and skills, cross-pollinating different capabilities and arts.

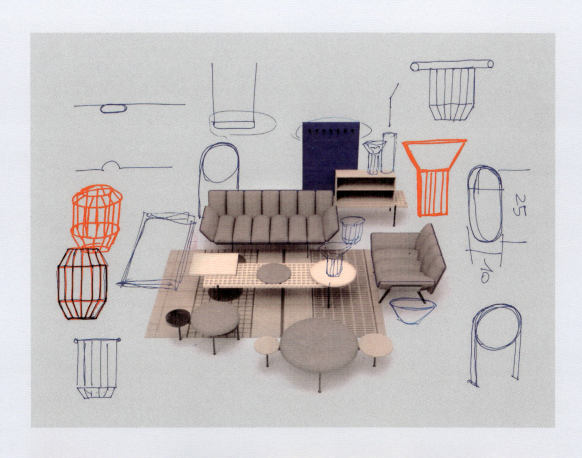

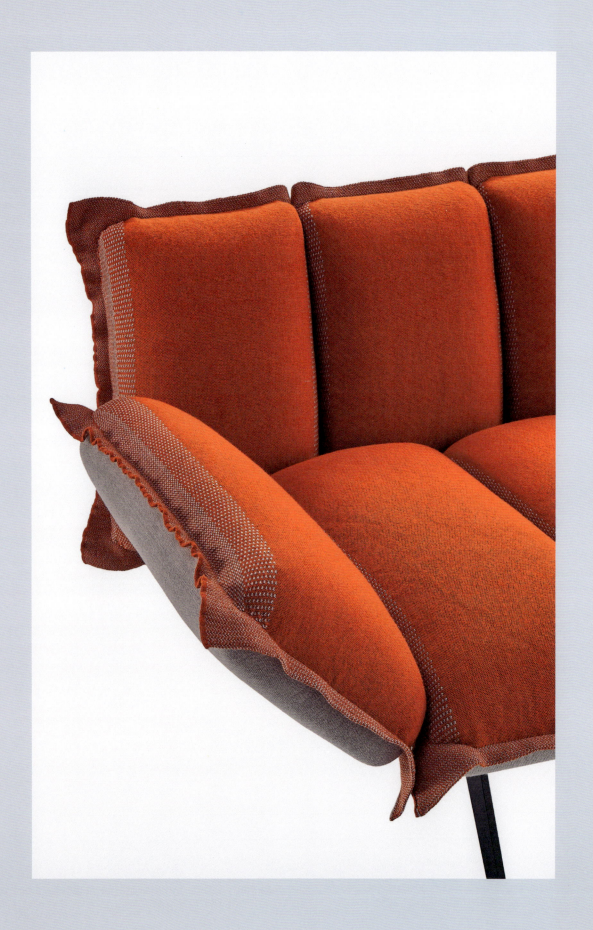

Type: Sofa System
Collection: Turati
Material: Fabric, Foam, Metal, Wood, Knitted textile, Upholstery
Colour: Various
Collaborator: Marie-Louise Rosholm
Team: Chloé Mestrude
Time: 2018
Client: Sancal

042. Arflex, Serena and Doge, 2014

Named after ancient terms for Venice and its leader, Serena and Doge are a bergère-style armchair and accompanying ottoman. They were inspired by classic Italian design and are made using traditional construction techniques, underscoring their connection with the fine craft of the past. Small enough to fit into domestic spaces, while still echoing the style and formality of the Ducal Palace in Venice, the armchair and ottoman bridge the historical and contemporary. →

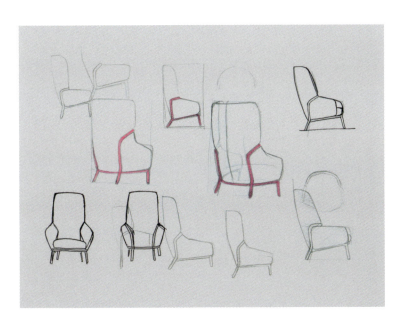

043. Hem, Hai, 2014

The Hai family is composed of a lounge chair and an ottoman that combine function with strong stylistic values, designed for the Hem brand of customizable furniture that is aimed at online retail. The lounge chair sits on a visually light metal structure, but features a gracefully curved padded backrest and armrests. The ottoman, also on metal legs, is elegantly minimal. The backrest folds forwards to make the armchair more compact for shipping. While being practical, Hai maintains comfort, style and a strong personality. →

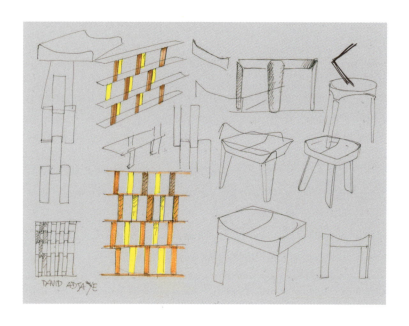

044. Mabeo, Pula, 2014

Produced in Botswana, the Pula family of side tables is named after the country's national currency. The series references coinage with its decorative border and frame, characterised by small incisions. Solid panga panga wood nesting coffee tables are laminated, shaped and milled by Mabeo craftspeople while the tiered system bookshelf with its elemental, framelike construction can also be used as a room divider or display shelf. →

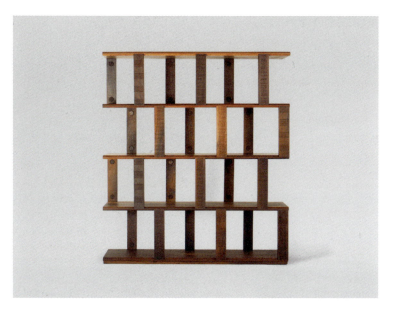

045.1 Mjölk, Aureola, 2014–16

The Aureola tea set has a curious shape, with all its elements piled up on top of one another like a totem. Designed in collaboration with Russian designer Lera Moiseeva, Aureola comprises a tea pot, a filter and two cups made from fine porcelain. Inspired by the round bowls used in Russian tea drinking and the beverage's ceremonial function in Asia, the set encourages communal drinking. →

045.2 Mjölk, Sucabaruca, 2014–16

Designed in collaboration with the Russian designer Lera Moiseeva, Sucabaruca is a coffee set that draws on the Scandinavian version of this contemporary ceremony. The porcelain set, which is composed of a tray, pot, filter and cups, is hand-etched and the tray's wooden or marble surface features its own unique patterns. The elements can be easily stacked and the conical pot echoes Armando Testa's 1960s cartoon character Carmencita. →

045.3 Mjölk, Uki, 2014–16

The glass diffuser of the Uki tea-light lamp appears to be a perfect globe, but its form has been carefully shaped to introduce subtle angles. While the diffuser is executed in Murano blown glass, Uki's base is produced out of spun brass made in Toronto, the materials and making processes revealing the quality of the manufacturing that lies behind the design. Uki gives off a soft and atmospheric light that illuminates any space. →

NO STITCHING IN UPHOLSTERY

MARIE-LOUISE ROSHOLM IN CONVERSATION WITH FRANCESCA PICCHI

No Stitching in Upholstery.
Marie-Louise Rosholm in conversation with
Francesca Picchi

Francesca Picchi: You experimented with Luca Nichetto on a knitted fabric for the covering of a sofa system. Working together you ended up with a series of inventions – innovations. Apart from introducing knitted fabrics into furniture, together you created a single piece that fits like a glove over a volume as large as a sofa. Can you tell us how you developed your research?

Marie-Louise Rosholm: I met Luca through a mutual friend. During my first visit to Nichetto & Partners' office in Porto Marghera, Luca confessed he was fixated on an idea. He wanted to have a type of sofa cover that would come finished from the loom and that without any further manual reworking, without needing to be stitched or cut, would fit perfectly over the structure.

The idea really captivated me. I started thinking about how to do it, because I have the kind of mind that loves challenges and then because this goal of developing a system according to a perfectly industrial logic connects with an interest in mechanical processes that I've always had. I like machines. So I began to think about ways to make it happen. Since I'm a pragmatic type and inclined to think by doing, I took out my sampling hand loom and set about trying to make it. The basic idea was to create pouches with openings. It was a rather complicated design with several overlapping layers, and in making the prototype, to understand these overlaps, I made things easier by using different colours. Then the colours became an important feature in determining the aesthetics of the project.

FP: Was it a long gestation?

MLR: The first prototype stayed on the shelf for about ten years while Luca was looking for a client willing to invest in producing a crazy project of this kind.

Finally Sancal entered the field, a Spanish company eager to experiment with new ideas. We made an appointment during the Salone del Mobile in Milan and pitched the idea to them. At first they had some misgivings, as they'd never produced a fabric of their own design – they usually chose fabrics ready-made from a catalogue. Anyway, they agreed.

So I began to do the rounds of the textile mills. In making the sample I had focused on a series of complications that I didn't know how to deal with on the loom. I talked about it to several textile experts. Some things promised well, others were less successful. One of these was the thickness of the upholstery of the sofa. Weaving could only make a fabric that would be quite thin. In recent years I had studied the seamless knitting technique for some garments. That gave me the insight, and I said to Luca, 'Why don't we knit it?'

The elasticity of knitting would solve most of the problems. And it had always been my dream to work with knitted fabrics for furniture. For a long time I had wanted to experiment in this field. What better opportunity than to do it with Luca!

The next step was to find a knitwear company willing to join in the experiment and able to translate the hand-woven prototype to study the technique and make it knitted. I got in touch with a Berlin knitting-machine agent, who referred me to a number of knitwear factories in Italy. I contacted them all. One sounded more intrigued than the others, so I decided to go and call on him. He was the right person. He took on the project and it was perfect. And everything went smoothly – almost – from then on.

FP: Had the manager of the knitwear factory ever done anything like it?

MLR: Never! It was all completely new to him. He was very helpful and ready to take on the project, partly because no one had ever seen anything like it.

FP: The type of research you did exemplifies a way of working directly with manufacturers and building a network in the prototyping phase typical of a certain strand of Italian design. Luca has made it his own and even exported it. How did this strike you?

MLR: I don't know whether it was something I already had in me or that I developed while working in Italy, but really getting my hands dirty and working directly with machines is a crucial part of my working method.

I need to build a network of people with different skills around me, and I bounce ideas off them to check whether I'm heading in the right direction and getting anywhere with the project. As a designer, I see my job as holding all the threads in my hand. I'm interested in bridging elements and I really like the idea of assisting cross-pollination. For our project, for instance, the meeting with the manager of the knitwear firm was decisive, because he developed a second prototype that was almost the industrially produced one-off piece ready to fit directly on to the structure that Luca was thinking of making. I took him my prototype made on the loom and Luca's drawing, and we talked about how to produce it, what we thought would be essential. A particularly difficult point to solve was the pouch where the padding is inserted, which has an asymmetrical design with the function of proportioning the whole. From the front it was clear that the line of separation between the two fabrics was not perfectly in the middle, because there was more fabric above than below. It wasn't easy to find the technical solution to this, but it was decisive in defining the form of the sofa.

Despite these technical complications, the whole prototyping process was pretty quick. Luca tweaked the design, the measurements, the proportions, even its modular concept and, for instance, the fact that the cover was removable, and finally the sofa took shape. When a lot of people are involved, it's good to keep the tension up so that the rhythm never flags.

FP: Next to textile design, colour is a crucial factor in your work. What criteria did you adopt?

MLR: We worked on the contrasts of deep, non-primary colours, and we worked on the nuances, or rather ways to soften the colours by mixing the yarns, to make it clear that it wasn't two pieces of fabric sewn together but a single knitted piece of material. At one juncture the colour points A and the colour points B migrate into each other, bringing out the way the same layer forms and changes function through the knitting process.

I know from experience that colour is extremely complex. The prime consideration is for it to be durable. From the point of view of sustainability there are several parameters to take into account, but the most important of all is to design things that last. If we're to consume less, we must be sure of what we're consuming. Above all, we have to change our outlook and no longer do things the way we did in the recent past.

It's no coincidence that the fabric is called Zero, with an allusion to zero waste, since no waste is produced and only the material necessary is used. It has received recognition for this important achievement.

FP: You lived for many years in Italy, so you're familiar with the network of small manufacturers willing to work experimentally. The project for Sancal is significant in this respect because in the development phase of the prototype you exchanged ideas with a whole series of people who assisted you in passing from the idea to the product. Since you come from a background with a very important tradition in design, Denmark, with its great strength in textiles, I'd like you to tell us about your experience.

MLR: Because of the way I work, it's essential to be at eye level with everyone involved and make sure that we're all on the same wavelength. This fact of having close at hand, all around you, a number of companies willing to experiment – as happens in Italy, at least in my experience – is something I haven't found anywhere else. Even just bringing a person like me, a designer, into the factory to work directly on the machines, from my thirty-five years of experience in the field, I can say that it's practically a unique situation.

My working method involves talking to people who don't have the same background as me, because that's the best way to get ideas. This is what happened when I was working with Luca. It was a complex project. We had to rise to a lot of challenges and we did it by getting together with all the people involved, combining the brainpower of the spinner of the yarn, the manager of the knitwear company, Luca's and mine. All these brains together managed to solve the most awkward problems. We hatched the project together, and we couldn't have done it by working alone. Collaboration is a great strength.

In my view, design is the method that enables you to connect worlds that otherwise would be separate. The designer's task is to join points that were never meant to meet.

Marie-Louise Rosholm is a Danish textile designer with significant experience in textiles and a special aptitude for research and innovation. She studied textile art and craft in Denmark and did her apprenticeship under Hanne Vedel, one of the most important Danish weavers, who worked with Finn Juhl and Hans J. Wegner. After developing in this tradition, in the 1980s Rosholm moved to Italy, where she stayed for some ten years, experimenting with textiles. In the mid-1980s she founded Studio MLR in Milan, and in 1992 she moved the business to Copenhagen. She is the founder of the Danish Color Board and president of Intercolor, an interdisciplinary platform for research and development in the field of colour. Today her research is mainly devoted to innovation in sustainability.

046. De La Espada, Elysia, 2014

A lounge chair that perfectly combines superb woodwork with bespoke tailoring. Its solid wood legs support an exceptionally comfortable backrest and seat. The chair's skeleton is exposed, rather than conventionally concealed, to showcase its fine materials and craftsmanship, as well as its generous proportions. As part of the Nichetto collection, Elysia's fusion of wood and other materials is inspired by the works of mid-century American architects. →

047. ZaoZuo Collection, 2015–18

ZaoZuo, which means 'design and production', is a young and dynamic Chinese design brand whose optimism matches that of China's nascent design culture. Luca Nichetto served as a creative director of this start-up furniture brand from 2015 to 2018. (See page 145.)

048. A. W. Bauer & Co., Ombra Delle 5, 2015

With a scent by Ben Gorham, Ombra Delle 5 is a perfume like no other, changing its character with the person who wears it. As befits this uniqueness, it is housed within a distinct bottle that is as extraordinary as the unisex fragrance it contains. By daylight, the bottle has a lilac hue, by night an incandescent lamplight changes it to blue. Handmade from irregular cuts of Murano glass, each bottle is entirely different. →

049. De La Espada, Blanche, 2015

The soft folds of this bergère-style armchair provide the perfect place for reading or private contemplation. Crafted in premium hardwood, with a choice of fabrics, Blanche has a soft seat and elegant wooden legs that are offset by two overlapping, tautly upholstered shells. Its enclosing form provides a feeling of privacy. In balancing handcrafted wood with luxurious fabrics, Blanche embraces French luxury and echoes the delicacy of form of mid-century furniture and architecture. →

050. De La Espada, Dubois, 2015

This elegant and timeless bed system creates a room within a room. Crafted from premium solid hardwood and a range of luxurious fabrics, Dubois features a generous expanse of upholstery. Integrated bedside tables are also available, while an optional wraparound headboard brings a sense of supreme comfort and privacy, making it suitable for residential or commercial environments. →

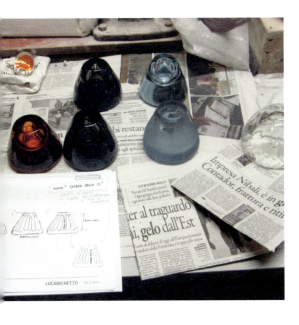

051. Arflex, Papoose, 2015

The perfect sofa should provide complete cosiness, letting its users feel safely enclosed within its structure. Named after a baby-carrier, Papoose is a modular sofa system that combines tailored upholstery detailing with complete comfort. →

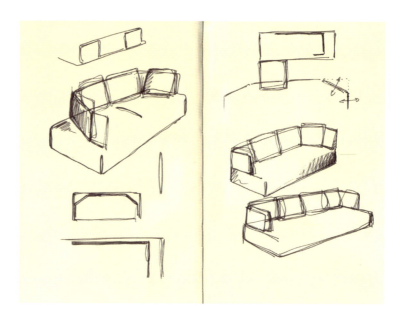

PROJECT 084
HERMÈS
PURE IMAGINATION

Project 084: Hermès, Pure Imagination, Venice

The experience of becoming a father has influenced my approach to design, pushing my imagination even further by simply observing my toddlers enjoying the pleasure of discovery and the power of whirlwind creativity they channel in every experience. Children notice what adults sometimes miss. Provided with a few wooden pieces, my son would imagine shapes and arrangements that I would never have conceived.

A journey through the toys, colours and textures of childhood memory was the key inspiration behind my first window-display project for Hermès' revamped Venice flagship store in 2018. As a young boy born in Venice and raised in Murano, the latter renowned internationally for its finest glassmaking tradition, I had developed a passion for Murano's mouth-blown glass techniques, which I wanted to embed in my first collaboration with the French luxury powerhouse.

When Natacha Prihnenko, international director of window display at Hermès, first approached me, she remembered fondly the Pyrae/Strata installation of totem-like, life-size figurines I had presented in partnership with Salviati in 2017. When I first got her email I was in Stockholm, and I flew straight to Venice to meet her at the iconic Caffè Florian on the city's Piazza San Marco. The theme for the following year's windows centred on playfulness under the tagline "Let's Play".

As Natacha detailed the design brief, everything clicked. I had the chance to involve Murano's glass artisans, all the while giving back stature to their artisanal technique, which had somehow become synonymous with keepsakes and touristic knick-knacks. As has been the case for other projects in my career, I relied on the expertise of several partners, from the glass expert Dario Stellon's Breaking the Mould, a glassmaking consultancy, to the artisans of the furnace company NasonMoretti and Luca Sacchi, who has long consulted for Hermès on window displays.

Hermès' windows are whimsical and dramatic, and used by the brand to champion artists and creatives by giving them a stage to showcase their work. I wanted my window display to reflect all that.

Taking my cue from board games, I envisioned a display consisting of a box of multicoloured objects with geometric shapes crafted from Murano mouth-blown glass, each boasting a different colour and texture inspired by the facades and interiors of Venetian palazzos. Mixed with iconic Hermès products, the display spurred the imagination by transforming the combination of elements into imaginary figures and fantasy places. Juxtaposed with one another they mimicked a steam train with its own locomotive and smoke, the latter evoked by an Hermès billowing silk Carré scarf, against an imposing yet playful skyline.

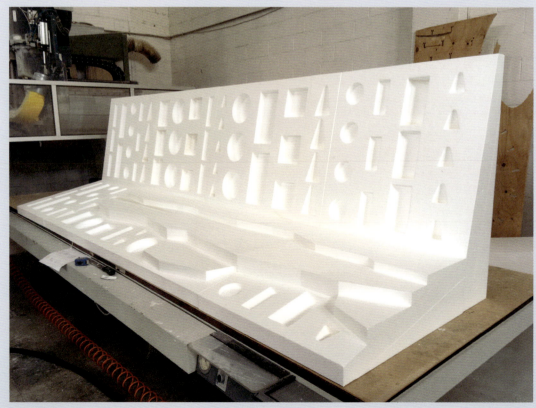

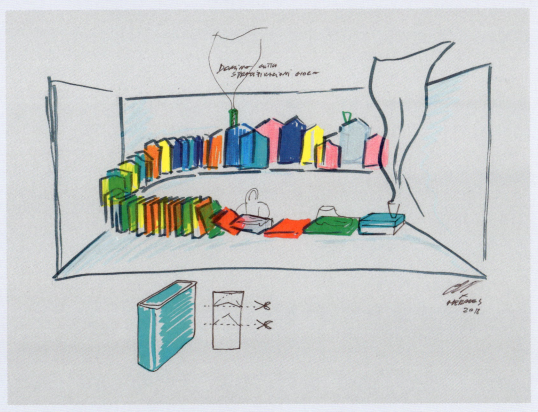

Type: Window Display
Material: Murano Glass, Metal, MDF
Colour: Various
Team: Chloé Mestrude
Time: 2018
Client: Hermès

052. De La Espada, Harold, 2015

With its tabletop drawer and compact proportions, the Harold writing desk evokes the era of letter-writing. The flat working area is surrounded on three sides by soft upward curves, and the H-frame legs and wedge tenons grant the table a breezy quality. The hardwood is hand-polished with lacquer for a subtle shine. Harold is a sleek, contemporary product, inspired by the past and drawing on De La Espada's expertise in crafting wood. →

053. De La Espada, Laurel, 2015

Composed of two pure geometric shapes, an intersecting cone and cylinder, this side table offers different tactility on each level. The solid, stable cone appears to float atop the base, in a fusion of form and function. Inspired by the balance of 1950s American architecture, Laurel is split equally between two materials, with stone or hardwood for the base and painted, hand-polished hardboard for the cone. →

POUFF
CABINET
TABLE

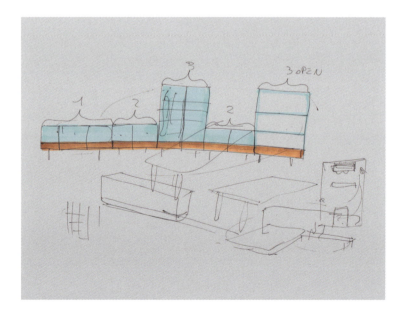

054. De La Espada, Marlon, 2015

An intriguing play of contrasts. Slender marble legs support a solid hardwood or marble tabletop, creating a robust structure that nonetheless creates an airy impression. The tabletop's numerous sections make it easily transportable, while resulting in a distinct and striking design detail. →

055. De La Espada, Mitch, 2015

Playing with ideas of display and concealment, the Mitch cabinet offers a selection of graceful yet efficient storage options. Its lightweight appearance belies its robust, solid wood structure. Small details such as the burnished brass door-pull, inspired by traditional Venetian doorbells, add character to the minimal design. Mitch's balance of handcrafted wood and complementary metal echoes the craft and form of American mid-century style. →

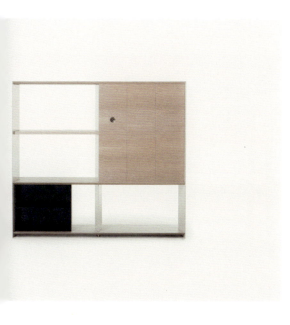

056. De La Espada, Stanley, 2015

A product of expert woodwork and joinery, the Stanley series of lounge furniture is crafted around an elegant exposed wooden frame that is upholstered with a choice of fabric. Taut upholstery provides a smooth finish to the backrest, while generously proportioned cushions give exceptional comfort. In balancing skilfully handcrafted wood with complementary fabrics, Stanley embraces the craftsmanship of America's great furniture and architecture of the 1950s. →

057. De La Espada, Vivien, 2015

A sculptural, solid wood chair whose form fuses the simple with the ornate, the machined with the handcrafted. Vivien's legs and stretchers are the product of traditional joinery, while its looped armrests and curved seat and backrest cultivate an elegant appearance. Vivien is the product of both CNC cutting technology and delicate hand-carving. →

GETTING CLOSE TO THE CULTURE
YOKO CHOY IN CONVERSATION WITH MAX FRASER

Getting Close to the Culture.
Yoko Choy in conversation with Max Fraser

Max Fraser: How did you meet Luca?

Yoko Choy: I knew Luca's name for a long time before we really got the chance to meet. We were introduced by Beatrice Leanza (see pages 137–140), who was creative director of Beijing Design Week at the time. But the first proper conversation we had was at the Venice Architecture Biennale in 2016. I was working with Beatrice on an exhibition in Venice, and Luca came by to have a look around the exhibition. It was then that we started our friendship. Because Venice is his home city, we toured local places, visited exhibitions and attended dinner parties.

MF: Back then, Luca was travelling to China a lot as part of his work for ZaoZuo. What was your observation of how he tackled that experience?

YC: Luca is always very open-minded. He had an openness in the way he tried to understand the culture, and he was working hard to create something new for that relationship he had formed in China. It was quite refreshing, because a lot of the time you see designers from abroad working in China for a local brand or local company, but you don't see anything particularly innovative. With ZaoZuo, Luca was trying to create a completely new concept for the Chinese market.

MF: More recently, you started working together. What sort of work are you doing?

YC: Since we met, we have always had a very honest discussion about design – about the industry or about the media, about trends, about sustainability, about Asia – and we always exchange ideas. We have a very good personal exchange as well; I don't call a lot of people I meet at work personal friends, but Luca is one.

Recently, Luca decided he wanted to transform the studio into more of a creative platform to take him beyond industrial design. I'm helping him on the messaging and also to produce content around his activities in order to move the studio in the direction of being a multidisciplinary design practice.

MF: Luca doesn't like to be defined or categorized. What is your impression of this?

YC: He doesn't want to be labelled a furniture or industrial designer, because he wants to be free to do things that he aspires to do. But there's a certain way that he wants to be perceived by the industry. Now he's trying to do more than just be a furniture designer or even an art director.

For example, as the art director of Wittmann, he is developing a programme to include a younger generation of designers from outside Europe, to introduce diversity and new energy to the company. As a successful designer, he doesn't have to nurture the next generation, or push bigger ideas about gender equality, sustainability, etc., but he is really putting effort into doing this. That is something I appreciate a lot.

MF: How would you describe the cultural or attitudinal differences between the design scene of China and that of Europe?

YC: If you think about China, the development and foundation of contemporary design is pretty much based on manufacturing – producing for and servicing foreign companies. This is how they have learned about contemporary design and gained experience and knowledge of design, and that is the position they have attained so far in the international design scene. What we understand about contemporary design now is very much based on Western culture. China doesn't have the same kind of history or environment yet to nurture an understanding of the value of design. I would say that's the fundamental difference between China and Europe.

Until very recently, there haven't been a lot of fruitful design collaborations between China and Europe. When they want to work with a foreign designer, it is often focused on a famous name that they use to communicate the product without really educating the market about design. You see a lot of these kinds of collaborations, but the outcome could only be economic. Designers who are interested in the market should invest in understanding the needs of the country or the cultural differences to decipher what we can improve and create together.

This is something Luca has done very well with ZaoZuo. He is willing to get really close to the culture and the people in order to understand the Chinese market. With his international experience, he asks what he can develop for the growing middle class in China, and strives to develop a brand that's suitable for China; this is exactly the collaboration we need, to really promote the value of design and to build something unique for the market and, in that sense, for the whole industry.

MF: What changes have you noticed in the design scene in China over the past decade?

YC: Even since Luca started working with ZaoZuo in 2014, the situation is already quite different. The younger Chinese generation have more international experience; a lot of them are educated abroad and then return to China to start their own businesses.

In Europe, you have a lot of design brands or companies who commission designers to do collections for them. But China has just adopted this model very recently; brands are being born out of the manufacturing skills and experience. China is no longer the cheapest place for production, much of which has moved to Southeast Asia. This has triggered a lot of factories to regenerate themselves and become brands in their own right. They're not as experienced as in Europe but nevertheless, they start working with younger local designers to try to build something new. Because of the manufacturing facilities available, a lot of young designers are also experimenting with their own products and starting up their own label. The industry structure is quite different.

Additionally, the situation in China is quite unique because the domestic market is so large. E-commerce is very developed and there are many channels for designers to reach local customers, that would already be enough to sustain their practice.

MF: What do you think is the general health of the design industry?

YC: As the world emerges from the Covid-19 pandemic, I've been talking to a lot of people and everyone is reflecting on their work and the way we over-produce and over-consume. I would love to prove myself wrong, but I'm not that optimistic about change. Certainly, environmental issues and the way we use resources are a huge challenge. But there has to be change, big change.

The whole conversation in the design industry is very Western-dominated; I would love to see more influences from not only the East but also everywhere else in the world. That kind of diversity is very important. Gender inequality is still a huge issue, too.

MF: What's your impression of the younger generations in relation to the ecological crisis?

YC: The younger generation definitely have a better understanding; they're more interested in this topic and seem to have a deeper connection with it. So, naturally, you see that reflected in their work. But the bigger brands need to be willing to lead the change in the industry. They have the responsibility but it's also important to educate the market and consumers to understand the value of design and quality.

MF: What have you learned from working with Luca?

YC: He's a great connector of people from every different discipline in the world, not only for work but also on a personal level. If he thinks two people could be good friends, he puts them together; people who can create good projects, he puts them together; he puts brands together, too. I don't think this is a skill that everyone has – it's unique. These kinds of collaborations and connections help everyone to understand the importance of working together and supporting each other. The genuine communication and relationships he builds around him are quite beautiful.

I remember attending the opening of Punta Conterie in Murano, which is a space to promote the island's industrial heritage and Italian culture. When I arrived there, I met Luca's whole family: his mother, his brother, his collaborators, the people he grew up with on the island, those he'd worked with in the glass factories, and many more. I was welcomed as though I was part of the family. To be there in that moment, in the place where he grew up, alongside people he holds close to his heart, to experience and share his blood connection … that was something that I cherish.

Since the beginning of her career, Yoko Choy has written about contemporary design for a variety of publications across the world. She currently works as the China editor for *Wallpaper** magazine, helping to bridge the gap between the international and China markets. Living between Amsterdam and her native Hong Kong, Yoko also advises design fairs, brands and design studios on their content and communication strategies, focusing particularly on those that are keen to enter the Chinese market, as well as Chinese companies wanting to expand globally. This cross-cultural liaison is carried out by her creative agency, *Collective Contemporist*, which she co-founded in 2018.

058. Foscarini, Kurage, 2015

Created in collaboration with Oki Sato of the Japanese design studio nendo, the Kurage lamp has a poetic simplicity that stands out wherever it is placed. Composed of natural materials – Japanese cypress-wood legs and a delicate washi-paper dome – it provides a soft glow and creates a gentle ambience. Although it is named after the Japanese word for jellyfish, it also resembles a scoop of ice cream, with the slender legs evoking lolly sticks. →

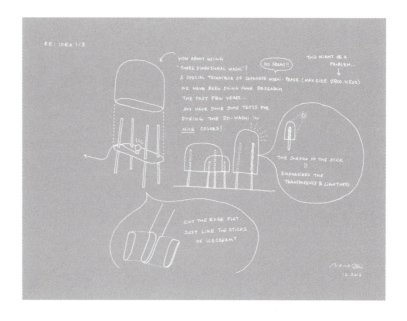

059. Hem, Alphabeta, 2015

This set of modular lamps is inspired by the way letters combine to form words. There are eight different shapes of shade, each of which is available in its own colour, as well as in both black and white. Twenty-four different configurations can therefore be created by combining top and bottom shades, with the potential for thousands more when four pendants are combined. Made from hand-spun metal, Alphabeta provides bi-directional lighting that brightens the space both above and below. →

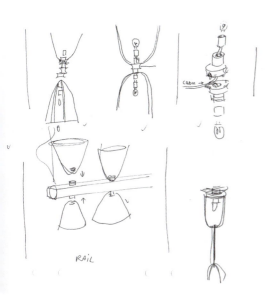

060. &Tradition, Cloud, 2015

Like its meteorological namesake, the Cloud family of seating appears to float above the ground. All pieces feature soft cushions atop an upholstered solid wood base, which is supported by elegant steel legs. This combination of defined form and generous comfort is a fusion of Danish and Italian design traditions, matching the Danish design brand &Tradition's values with Luca Nichetto's vision. →

061. Arflex, Algon, 2016

When Luca Nichetto was commissioned by the esteemed Italian brand Arflex to design club furniture, he took inspiration from the company's heritage and experimental manufacturing processes. Melding Scandinavian simplicity with a patterned, quilted upholstery designed by Luca, Algon is strictly formal, while offering soft comfort. →

062. Arflex, Capilano, 2016

Supported by a light, elegant metal frame, the Capilano table system takes its name from the Capilano Suspension Bridge in Vancouver. Originally developed to complement the Papoose sofa that Luca Nichetto also designed for Arflex, Capilano is a standalone series of coffee and side tables available in numerous configurations: square, triangular and rectangular. While the frame is metal, the tabletop is made of wood, marble or Laminam, a high-tech porcelain tile with a smooth, resistant surface. →

PROJECT 073
SALVIATI
PYRAE/STRATA

Project 073: Salviati, Pyrae/Strata

When I was twenty-three years old and in my final years at Venice's architecture university IUAV studying industrial design, Simon Moore – who in 1999 was the art director of the glassmaker Salviati – agreed to buy some sketches from my portfolio out of courtesy, despite them not having much commercial viability. Salviati is the company I always reference when I am asked why I decided to become a designer, and although that initial interaction with Moore could have seemed like an empty gesture, that seminal contact would spawn a future collaboration with the company I had so long admired.

My family history is intertwined with Murano's art of mouth-blown glassmaking, not only because I grew up on the island and was accustomed to seeing a sketch being turned into glassware daily, but also because both my grandfathers and my mother used to work in the industry.

In 1999 the glass expert Dario Stellon – who at that time worked for Salviati – called me to say that Simon was looking for young talents skilled at and keen on CAD. I joined the company, and was offered an opportunity to experience at first hand the business's requirements and hurdles.

Without knowing it, I was about to follow in the footsteps of acclaimed designers and artists such as Ingo Maurer, Anish Kapoor, Ross Lovegrove and Tom Dixon with my first project for the company, the Millebolle vase collection (see page 14) featuring large air bubbles embedded in the glass paste through an experimental technique mastered by a skilled glazier. It launched in 2000 and became one of the bestselling collections for the brand.

In 2015 the fruitful relationship with Salviati was reprised, adding yet another notch on my belt. After the company changed ownership, Dario – who had been a fixture for my entire personal and professional life – came knocking at the door, committed to putting the brand back on the international design map.

I am not a solitary designer, and my studio and external collaborators always inspire my design practice. For this project I started an exchange with my friend Ben Gorham, founder of the perfume house Byredo, relating to his holistic vision and pledging to research new possibilities for traditional glassmaking and craftsmanship. Our mesmerizing installation at the Decode/Recode event space, presented in two adjoining warehouses in the heart of Milan's Ventura Centrale district, took Milan Design Week 2017 by storm and became viral among attendees and on social media.

The Pyrae hall was populated by fifty-three illuminated totems, formed by stacking mouth-blown glass elements as an elaboration on the ancestral, doll-like representation of the human body and a reflection on the multicultural world we live in. It was connected to the Strata hall, a study in modularity, through the layering of delicate glass elements into imposing towers that recalled stacked books, showcasing the potential for organizing a single piece into a colossal composition.

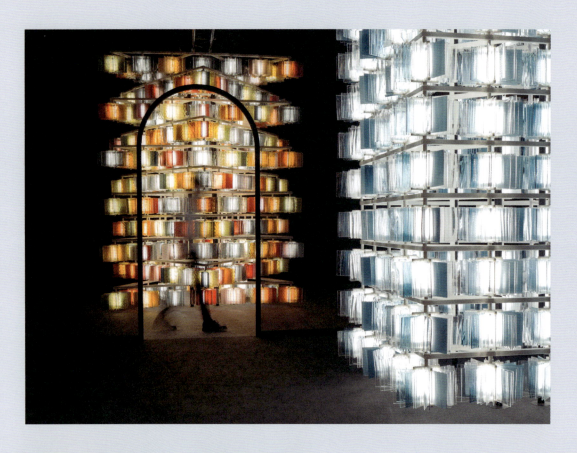

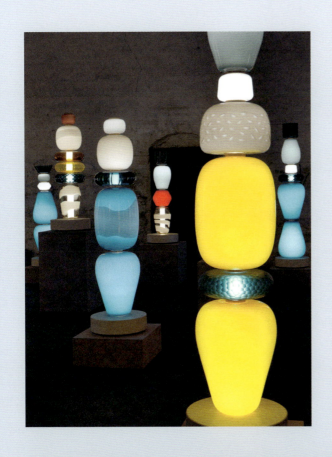

Type: Exhibition/Installation
Material: Glass
Colour: Various
Collaborator: Ben Gorham
Team: Daniele Caldari
Time: 2017
Client: Salviati

063. De La Espada, Kim, 2016

Available as a set or as standalone pieces, the three items in the Kim family share materials, while having their own distinct forms. Simple but with a strong sense of character, the pieces have beautifully finished wooden surfaces that straddle the boundary between natural and manmade. →

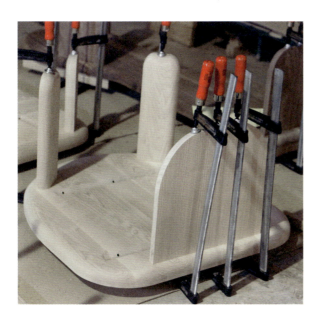

064. De La Espada, Nino, 2016

When it launched in 2014, the Elysia lounge chair was the first product in the Nichetto collection for De La Espada. In 2016 it was joined by Nino, an ottoman that shares its stylistic principles. Nino matches Elysia perfectly, as well as complementing the other items in the Nichetto collection. Its solid wood skeleton is exposed rather than concealed, showcasing its fine material and craftsmanship, while its fusion of wood and upholstery is inspired by mid-century design. →

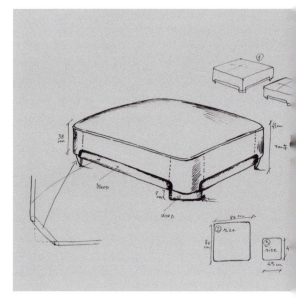

 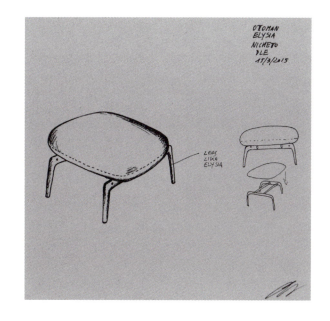

065. De La Espada, Steve, 2016

Gemstones set into jewellery were the starting point for Steve, a series of upholstered poufs for Luca Nichetto's eponymous furniture collection for De La Espada. It has short cast-iron legs that support visible wooden structures crowned with upholstery, and is available in three sizes. Perfect as a standalone piece, Steve can also complement the Blanche, Stanley and Elysia chairs. It continues the Nichetto collection's aim of combining heritage styling with contemporary design. →

066. Ethimo, Esedra, 2016

Inspired by elements of Classical architecture, Esedra is a family of contemporary outdoor furniture. The union of aluminium and teak with synthetic fabric upholstery retains an artisanal sensibility and the warmth typical of natural, woven fibre. The resulting collection is refined yet welcoming and enhances the pleasure of being outdoors. →

067. NasonMoretti, Halo, 2016

With its two connecting components, the lamp echoes the form of a wine glass, subtly suggesting the act of drinking. A coloured opaque base sits under a larger transparent top, which is available in several patterns. As well as being ornamental, these patterns transform the nature of the light emitted by the lamp. As the patterns overlap, they form complex motifs, creating a decorative quality that shines through even when the lamp is off. →

068. Offecct, Phoenix, 2016

The product of two years of research and refinement, the Phoenix chair is named after the immortal firebird of Greek myth. Its name conveys its sustainability: if a part is damaged, it can be easily replaced with a new one, while the old part can be safely disposed of and recycled. Phoenix turns structural simplicity into a striking aesthetic, and the bold curve of the back and seat provides all-important comfort. →

THE ORIGIN: MURANO AND GLASSMAKING

DARIO STELLON IN CONVERSATION WITH FRANCESCA PICCHI

The Origin: Murano and Glassmaking.
Dario Stellon in conversation with Francesca Picchi

Francesca Picchi: To get a more vivid idea of the context of glassmaking on Murano, Luca Nichetto suggested I ask you about the world you two grew up in. This is not just because you've known each other since you were kids, but also because you're one of the leading experts in glassmaking in Murano. I personally have the impression that you invented a profession that can be considered the contemporary version of the *maestro* glassmaker. Is this idea right?

Dario Stellon: I wouldn't say that, because a *maestro* glassmaker has a whole range of technical knowledge and above all does the physical work, fashioning glass directly using manual skills and know-how in a symbiotic relationship with the material, while I deal with production in a more mediated way. I'm interested in creating a network of relationships to make production possible. I like to see it as a work of translation.

My family's history, like that of almost all the families on Murano, has always been bound up with glass. Everyone on the island thinks in terms of the same material, and glass production leaves its mark on people's lives and actions. It's the milieu itself that naturally transmits a whole range of knowledge. Despite its small population, this little world thrives because of its international connections. The centrality of glass is palpable and inevitably shapes your formative years.

Fortunately glass is a constantly evolving material and there's always room for innovation. From the point of view of a designer – and this is what happened to Luca – the continuous scope for discovering something new encourages the effort to extend the limits of the material. In this respect, the prospect of placing the skill of glassmakers at the service of new projects is a stimulus to think continually about possible new applications.

FP: Is that what you do when you work together?

DS: Luca and I spent our early years together, and the ties between us are not just our work but a long-standing friendship. The first real work we did together was at Salviati, when Luca designed his first product, the Millebolle vase [2000]. At the time I was the firm's in-house production manager and the art direction was handled by Simon Moore. Together we urged Luca to design something for Salviati, and he came up with a vase that was an immediate success and is still an icon of the company, one of the most representative brands in Murano's history.

FP: Why do you think it was such a success?

DS: The insight lay in adopting a traditional technique and modifying it by introducing an element of difference to bring the form up to date. I'd say this is a thread running through all Luca's work: rewriting elements of tradition in a contemporary key.

In the case of the vase, it was a question of reinventing the traditional technique of a bolle glass, which produces a special decorative effect by creating small air bubbles trapped inside a thick mass of glass. Luca's invention was to lighten the perception of the glass mass, blowing the vase to dilate the bubbles so they seem to be floating in air. As I said, it was a commercial success. Beyond the artistic qualities, marketability is a crucial component and Luca is particularly good at it.

FP: What do you mean by marketability?

DS: Marketability means, for instance, that all the problems are solved on paper, before the product goes into the furnace. Glass leaves no margin for adjustments outside the furnace. If you work with wood, iron or marble you can retouch them in the finishing phase, but with glass you never get a chance to correct errors made in the first stage. If you make a mistake, you have to start again. For this reason, you have to rely on the expert hands of the glassmakers and build a relationship of mutual trust. This is where my role comes in, which includes selecting the companies and craftspeople capable of developing individual projects by their skills. There are a lot of techniques, and choosing the right pair of hands is important, as is understanding how to industrialize a product (although I use this term, we're obviously talking about pure craftsmanship).

It's less romantic than people think. Glass requires you to have clear ideas about what you want to achieve. I think it's a good school.

FP: What would you say are the most significant projects that you and Luca have worked on together?

DS: As I mentioned, my training was connected with glass because of my family background. I started working in the family business, Serenella Industria Vetraria, then moved to Venini, and shortly afterwards I joined Salviati, where I worked for twenty-one years. When the company was taken over by a new owner in 2017, we needed to relaunch the brand. I asked Luca for help in realizing the potential of the project with a company that was ready to use its knowledge on a technical level and its production capacity to tackle large-scale projects and enter the contract sector.

It was an ambitious project, and we spent months together designing and working out all the details. In April 2017 they took the result of our work to Milan, during Design Week, with an installation in the connected warehouses of the Central station. We produced 53 totemic objects by assembling 102 modules with different shapes, colours and production methods. In theory they could be combined to make more than ten thousand original compositions, each different from the others. I could describe it as a sort of reinterpretation of the Terracotta Army, but made entirely of glass. It was an incredible effort, and Luca and I shared the desire to display, if not all, then at least as many glassworking techniques as possible, an immense range of possibilities. This work paved the way for even more ambitious projects, such as creating whole glass landscapes with a great visual impact for Hermès's window displays, first for its store in Venice [2018], and later for the one in Hong Kong [2019]. On these occasions we worked very closely with the glassmakers, who shaped the numerous elements of different colours and finishes in the Murano glassworks, to be shipped for assembly in China.

FP: Can you explain how glassmaking is organized in Murano?

DS: The glassworks are organized by teams of people working together, called *piazzas*. In Murano, traditionally, the *maestro* glassworker has the crucial task of organizing a *piazza*. Keeping a company's costs down depends on the number of pieces the team can make and the time they take. This means the organization of the *piazza* has to be perfect. It has to be a perfectly synchronized mechanism. Everyone has an essential task in keeping with a centuries-old pattern of linked actions, and each has a specific name: the *maestro*, the *servente*, the *serventino*, the *leva-paline*, the *leva-pareson*.

You could say that the Murano *maestro* glassmaker always used to be trained in an industrial type of organization. Then the narrative developed through marketing that began to be aimed at tourists, who arrived on the island to see how glass was made, and this led the *maestro* glassmakers to become more like artists. Partly for this reason the role of design is a fundamental stimulus for this group of glassworkers, especially today, when many of them have lost their connection with design.

Traditionally, the most extraordinary things were created only when the *maestro* glassmaker was able to put all the wisdom of the team at the service of art or design. And this, as I see it, is the model that still needs to be reproduced in Murano, to try and strengthen the research that smaller companies are struggling to do.

FP: Is this what led you to create BTM, or Breaking the Mould, a working party to conduct research and experimental projects on Murano glass?

DS: The project grew out of the relationship with Luca and the many artists and designers I have met through my work. When I left Salviati, I realized there was a lack of people capable of supervising this work of translation for the community on Murano, which had enormous potential but seemed unable to fulfil it. I met people guided by similar ideas and we decided to come together as a team. For me, being born in Murano, it's easy to recognize the contradictions in a system and understand the ways to try and correct them.

FP: In a way, you're inspired by what Paolo Venini did when he made a change in production on Murano, adding the contribution of famous designers alongside the historic figure of the *maestro* glassmaker.

DS: This is one of the things that prompted me to found BTM. With Luca, as children, we spent many evenings playing with glass, and as adults we found ourselves talking and thinking through the problems. I guess we share the goal of attracting work to Murano to try to stimulate a certain type of quality production through far-sighted projects. We share a faith in the enormous potential of this community, a true culture.

I've had opportunities to visit a lot of companies in the Veneto, where the quality of production continues to surprise me and the quality of relationships should be nurtured and kept alive. Italy is a microcosm of businesses whose value needs to be enhanced by a type of work, which I call translation, to enable them to fulfil their potential. I think networking and the ability to create synergy are what we need most. All artisanal production districts experience the same problems: a touch of parochialism, a little difficulty in scaling production up to the new dimensions of the market or making companies more open and internationalizing them.

I'm really confident that design can perform the task of raising awareness. It's crucial to keep up a dialogue between businesses and designers, and the search for the new, for beauty, for innovation, acts as a driving force that companies are not always able to produce internally, but it can make a difference. The only way to preserve tradition is by innovating.

With over twenty years of experience as a glass expert and as the production manager of some of the most renowned glassmaking firms on Murano, Dario Stellon is considered one of the leading authorities in the field of glass production. In 2011, in collaboration with others from various professional backgrounds, Stellon started an experimental project on Murano glass. Called Breaking the Mould (BTM) it explores the production processes and seeks to identify possible technological innovations in a process that is still predominantly traditional. BTM aims to combine research and experimentation with productive and creative consulting for companies and freelancers.

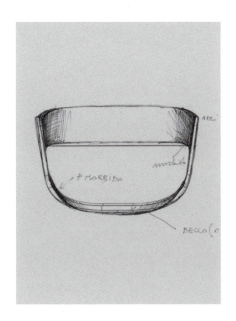

069. &Tradition, Isole, 2017

Two designers from different cultures, Luca Nichetto and nendo, co-created the modular Isole virtually via a process of exchanging ideas inspired by Japanese poetry. The outcome is Isole, Italian for 'islands', a truly unique sofa concept enabling a variety of combinations and configurations, including versions with and without an 'island' arm cushion. Variations include a discreet round, square or rectangular side table that integrates beautifully with the overall aesthetic. →

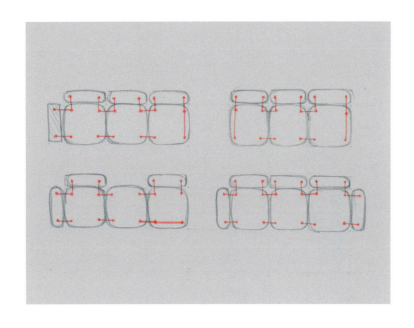

070. Artifort, Pala, 2017

Like a shell moulded around its inhabitant, Pala is a lounge chair that wraps around the body, offering a uniquely cosy experience. The pleasantness of its structure, with a core of metal and upholstered foam covered in textile of various colours, was designed to embrace the desire of maintaining a relatively small size while preserving comfort. The quality is enhanced by the matching ottoman that conceals a tiny storage space under its top. →

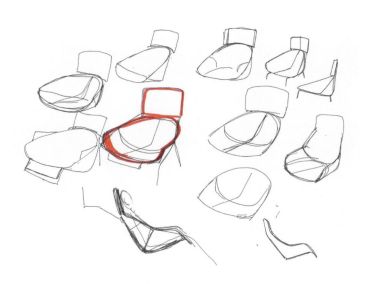

071. Coedition, MDW Stand, 2017

This stand was conceived as a compendium of the company's visual identity. The space was divided into four areas chromatically, with several colours sectioning off floor and walls. Partitions of the corresponding colour mark each perimeter without blocking the view across the entire stand. In balance with the tones and images featured in Coedition's collection, every area represents a unique experience for the visitor, who gets to walk through a series of home-inspired set-ups. →

072. Coedition, You, 2017

The creative process behind this sofa for Coedition aimed to emphasize the dimensions and thickness of the armrests and backrest. In the manner of a big, soft glove that holds the user in its palm, the You sofa offers a unique experience in comfort. The large seat and the roundness of the spherical back avoid any postural stiffness in favour of a freer sitting position, and the variety of materials and colours makes the sofa easily adaptable for residential or commercial environments. →

073. Salviati, Pyrae/Strata, 2017

Set up in the spaces of a warehouse in Milan city centre, the Pyrae/Strata installation invites visitors through an immersive experience to observe a series of unique mouth-blown objects designed and crafted specially for the event. A play of light and materials characterizes the Strata hall, where three compositions of glass layers stand between walls of translucent textile. The Pyrae hall contains a multitude of lighting objects made of stacked glass elements and showcased on fifty-three podiums. (See page 103.)

LUCA NICHETTO: FOUR INTERVIEWS WITH MAX FRASER

Venice, Stockholm, not Milan

Max Fraser: You were born in Venice, raised on the neighbouring island of Murano, studied in Venice and set up your first design studio there – it's fair to say that Venice was the epicentre of your life! So, what was your perception of Milan, which is usually considered the epicentre of design in Italy?

Luca Nichetto: The first time I went to Milan was in 2000, when Foscarini launched my first lamp, which I had designed with Gianpietro Gai. I was there to attend a presentation as a designer of an actual product, not only as a student. I was not a big fan of the city; it was too crowded for me. I was in a very comfortable zone in Venice, and with a couple of projects with Salviati and others for Foscarini, I had the chance to open up my little studio in Venice. It was owned by me and I loved it. Because of the education I had had from the beginning of my career, I was working a lot with suppliers in my region of Veneto. These suppliers had sort of become my agents, as they were making parts for companies across different sectors and they would often act as the link for me to potential clients. Before I knew it, I was in contact with companies like Moroso and Kristalia that were part of the Venice region. So, whenever I had the feeling that I should move to Milan because of the design scene there, I would ask myself, why?

I had this feeling that Milan was Milan, a sort of bubble, and everything outside it was kind of foreign. I always felt like an outsider. I had enough opportunities in my own region. Very quickly, I could see that I could still live in my own city, where there's plenty of local industry and production, it's much easier and more convenient for me, and it's an environment that I like. So that's what I did! In the following years, as I attracted the attention of journalists, there was a curiosity from them about this young designer from Venice.

I remember the designer Fabio Novembre gave me some good advice – he said, 'If you're in Venice, you're the only one. If you're in Milan, you're one of many.' He gave me the confidence to stay in the city that I grew up in and that I love. I like to think I showed younger designers that it's possible to do this job without needing to be in a major hub. You can find the opportunities around you if you look with different eyes.

MF: What made you turn your attention to Sweden?

LN: This was a connection with my private life. In 2003 I met my future wife, Åsa, in Venice and started to visit Sweden quite often with her. We would return for her birthday, which coincided with the Stockholm Furniture Fair in February. I started to explore the fair and spotted furniture brands such as Offecct and Swedese that were open-minded about working with international designers.

And then I said to myself, OK, I will try to work abroad, because if I feel that the Milan community perceives me as a foreign person, I might as well pursue opportunities further afield. And Sweden was a logical target, because I was travelling there anyway. So I went to the fair in February 2007 and met Anders Englund, the co-founder of Offecct. My English was terrible, yet we managed to communicate with our hands! There was a good chemistry, he invited me to visit the company and then he set me a brief. It was the first time I had worked for a company abroad, allowing me to compare the similarities and differences of working with an Italian company.

MF: At what point did you feel you were turning a corner in your career?

LN: That moment was 2010, when I designed the Robo chair for Offecct (see page 217). Anders gave me the opportunity to showcase the chair and some of my other designs for other companies in Offecct's showroom in central Stockholm. I think that was the moment that the big Italian companies turned their eyes to my work and wondered, who is this young Italian designer working abroad? And that was the first time Cassina approached me, De Padova, Molteni … that is what got the ball rolling.

MF: So you had to go out of Italy in order to come back in. Before that, did you feel there were obstacles to working with the Italian brands?

LN: There were a lot of Italian designers of my generation who were living under the shadow of the three previous generations. The old masters such as [Achille] Castiglioni, [Vico] Magistretti and [Ettore] Sottsass were working with the best companies, then the next generation – the 'new masters' such as [Antonio] Citterio, [Piero] Lissoni and [Rodolfo] Dordoni – also had to establish themselves, but they did so with the younger companies, such as Minotti, Poliform and Living Divani, which were new in the 'big league'. That generation invented the role of art director for these brands, designing everything for them: identity, showrooms, advertising, etc. Then there was the generation just below them, such as [Fabio] Novembre, [Carlo] Colombo and [Roberto] Palomba, who had the problem of finding their place amid the older competition. And then there was my generation, who had to push through three generations in order to get in. It was clear to me that I couldn't focus my energy on that congested part of the industry; I needed to find something else.

MF: But as well as the older generations of Italian designers, there were also Italian producers starting to work with foreign designers as a way of expanding their international appeal.

LN: Yes, Philippe Starck was one of the first to open that door, and he changed a lot. I remember when the Bouroullec brothers came on the scene, these two French designers were pretty young; Erwan Bouroullec is the same age as me. I was looking at them and they were working with brands like Cappellini, Magis and Kartell, but I didn't consider that to be a problem. For me, that was an indication that I could take a similar approach in other countries.

I compare it to sport – Italy was the top league in design and I was grateful to be born in that country. But for me to play in that league, I required experience and to practise abroad in order to get back in; if I stayed focused only on Italy, it would be harder to grow from the minor league.

MF: So would you say your approach made you more exotic to those Italian companies?

LN: I think it probably triggered their curiosity at the beginning. It gave me the freedom to be an outsider who didn't need to play by any rules of the game. I didn't realize that immediately; I was not so strategic. I think it was more like a gut feeling or pure luck! Perhaps it is the luck that came from trying to do the best for my private life and never the opposite. And I still think in that way today.

MF: With that said, in 2010 Åsa was offered a good job in Stockholm and moved back to her native city. You told her you would follow, and in 2011 you set up a studio in Stockholm and kept your Venice studio going as well, travelling between the two. What were the noticeable cultural differences for you?

LN: Sweden taught me to feel less pressure in terms of performing as a designer. When you grow up in Italy, the focus is often on how good things once were, and doesn't often look to the future. I think this is a problem for Italy in general; we are spoiled by the rich legacy left by the visionary people who came before us. When I moved to Sweden, I didn't have that kind of pressure. I do what I want to do and I try to rid myself of this idea that every time I pick up a pen, I need to design an icon.

That new attitude helped me to clean up my mindset and observe different cultures with a lot more curiosity. Different countries see opportunity in different things, and that helped to push me out of my comfort zone, to challenge myself and stretch my own creativity. It was sort of liberating.

MF: Do you feel you're now part of the design club of Stockholm?

LN: No, I don't, and I feel very proud of that. Whenever I feel that is happening I take five steps away, because I like my position as an outsider, not depending on a 'scene'. The most beautiful thing about this job is to have the freedom to decide what you do and don't want to do, to choose who you want to work with and then not worry about being judged for that. I have the privilege of being able to jump into opportunities that challenge me and my studio in different scenarios.

Even the word 'designer' I find too prescriptive. In Italian we have the word *proggettista*, but there isn't an equivalent in English. It describes a person who is working on many projects for people; that could be dresses, objects, food, environments, whatever. The word 'designer' immediately puts you in a box, and then we add prefixes such as 'industrial', 'fashion', 'lighting' ... I think if you're doing many projects, it allows you to be more rounded in your approach.

If I was too much part of a defined community, I would need to play by some rules, but I don't like rules. Of course, I need to respect some of them, but I don't like it when people put a stamp on me.

The Business of Design

MF: How have you seen the business of design changing in the time you've been working?

LN: At the beginning of my career, I was so naïve in terms of business. First of all, I'd never worked in another studio, so I was jumping straight from university to a freelance position. The first thing I heard about was royalties as the basic payment set-up for designers. Royalties were a beautiful discovery for me because I realized that you continue to get paid for work you've already done, like a passive income.

From 2000 to 2008, when I was working as a freelancer, royalties made up one hundred per cent of my income. It was sustainable because I was lucky enough to work with the right companies – Salviati and Foscarini – and they were still growing, so there was always a consistent amount of royalties coming to me. At that time, contracts were based on the standard contracts that were published by ADI [the Association of Industrial Design], which would also provide mediating services in case of any disputes. But these contracts were mostly written in favour of the producer, rather than the designer.

When I had the opportunity to meet other designers, I was always curious about how they structured their income. I discovered that you could not only earn via royalties but also charge a fee for the project. This was also the moment when I started to realize the lack of education at university on these business matters; they were focused on teaching you how to design beautiful products, but nobody was preparing us for how we could survive from this job! We needed to know about the different kinds of contract, the royalty model, fees, copyright, etc. I think it is probably one of the most important parts to teach, so as to prepare young people for what they face when they jump into the industry.

MF: That is certainly a criticism I've heard across the world. When you started out, you were young, you had low overheads and few responsibilities, so perhaps you had little reason to question the royalty model.

LN: Yes, for me it was a bonus and I was having the best life ever; I had royalties from Salviati and a fee working as an external R&D consultant for Foscarini, which was my bread and butter. I had a lot of freedom, also in the way I chose to structure my time. And then the moment came when my turnover was going up and I was spending a lot of money on taxes, so my accountant suggested I invest some of it as a way of lowering my tax bill. I decided to start a company and to buy a property to house my design studio. I was thirty and maybe still naïve enough to jump into that and just figure it out as I went along!

I remember there were some journalists who used to tease me because I knew the turnover of different brands in Italy. I wanted to know this because my responsibilities were growing and I needed to build my universe; I was not only interested in the beauty of their products but also in their turnover, because it gave me a pretty clear idea of the direction they were heading. Then I could assess if they could be a solid client later on. For me it was a way of understanding the industry – if I wanted to build a sustainable business with a proper margin, I needed to consider all these aspects of my clients. I was curious, I asked questions and this helped me to piece together the puzzle and formulate my own approach.

MF: So was this the moment when you started to ask for a fee for projects?

LN: Yes, and when I started to ask for a fee, most of the companies told me that they only work with royalties. I began to understand how much a company was interested in the project in relation to how much they were willing to invest in me. In the beginning, most of the companies were not paying me a fee but offered advance royalties instead. Of course, it was up to me to decide if that worked or not, but it was the first time I figured out what it means to negotiate.

Also, I realized pretty early that if I was the person speaking to my client about creativity at the same time as I was speaking about money, it would never work. It creates a confusing dynamic. I started to ask around and fellow designers advised me to work with a good lawyer for these financial and contractual matters. I think that gave a more structured perception of me to the client, and I started to get more fee-based work, not just advance royalties. At the same time I observed my lawyer's negotiating methods, which was helpful. It felt as though we were starting to achieve the right value for the work we were doing, in consideration of the time involved and prior experience. I was then thinking like a company to ensure that we were able to cover salaries and overheads every month and earn a decent margin for our activities. Quite often, the fee doesn't cover the time involved, but the royalties will hopefully close that gap. Strategically, I could then assess how many projects we would need to undertake every year, together with an analysis of the financial timeline.

MF: As well as the design work, what other elements were clients asking you to work on?

LN: I was also accountable for other aspects of a project, working as a sort of consultant at one moment, then a copywriter, then a social-media communicator, then joining the press machine … Of course, all these 'extras' have a value. The companies tell you that you will benefit from a lot of press coverage, but they also need you to generate a lot of press for them! And then you realize that there are companies coming to you because of your media profile as much as for the quality of the work you are doing.

MF: Yes, I remember at Milan Design Week in 2011, I was part of a campaign called #milanuncut, which aimed to expose the exploitative nature of the royalty system – not only were designers receiving a low percentage, but also they were expected to fulfil all these extra roles as part of it.

LN: Yes, I remember that year well. There was a kind of taboo involved – not many designers wanted to talk publicly about those issues, perhaps because they thought it might upset their existing and potential clients.

Royalty agreements haven't changed, but the realities of the market have. For example, as Italy's industry emerged after World War II, the designers at that time found a way to get paid with a royalty of three per cent. It is worth remembering that there weren't as many producers then and there weren't as many designers either, so they had a sort of monopoly and the three per cent was enough.

At the beginning this was calculated from direct sales, but then it was calculated from the wholesale price, which is usually fifty per cent less than the direct sale price. And then, as the market grew and became more competitive, the sales teams became more and more important and would be earning higher commission than that paid to the designer. The value system shifted so that design was not as important as sales. A sales agent typically receives seven to ten per cent commission, and if the designer asks for the same, the finances don't work. And then the sales agents started to add more and more products to their portfolios, which dilutes the likelihood of your product being chosen by the buyer …

MF: Why hasn't anything changed in that regard?

LN: I think designers are kind of stuck in that way of working because nobody takes a stand. We should talk to each other and try to find a proper way for all of us to work, otherwise we will be in trouble. But there is always someone who doesn't care about that and will accept a lower royalty because they need the work or they're trying to establish themselves quickly. There is not really a way to manage that.

MF: How else has the role of a designer changed?

LN: It has changed drastically in the last fifteen years [since 2005]: the number of products we design; the superficiality of what the companies want; some design has become a cosmetic tool to sell other things; the demand for speed that creates rushed products … At first I didn't like the exploding demands on design studios, but the truth is, that is an evolution of the job and you can't fight it; you must understand the evolution of where things are moving and try to keep the roots of what you love doing, while all the time adapting to the future.

MF: How have you adapted to these changes?

LN: Seeing where things were moving, I started to think, if I want to be able to do my job properly, I can't only be a designer recognized for a chair or a lamp. I needed to expand the scope of what I was doing and make it visible and profitable. I started thinking that I needed to balance the royalty work with fees, strategic work and consultancy, then look at the job from 360 degrees. You cannot stay with your head stuck in the ground, spending five years developing a chair – that'll never work. You need to be sustainable on the business side.

So there was a moment when I started thinking, Nichetto Studio is no longer just Luca Nichetto – I needed to embrace the collective nature of a studio and one that provides different services to my clients. We were doing a lot of these services already, without clients knowing, but when I made them visible, I started to see a lot of requests coming in. That helped us to balance things and move away from royalties providing one hundred per cent of our income to where we are now, which is about forty per cent. It didn't happen overnight.

MF: You've now assumed the role of art director for certain companies, where you're no longer just responsible for designing new products but are also undertaking several other elements of the brand's identity and direction. What is that experience like?

LN: I've learned a lot. I love to do art direction where I'm not the only player, because I don't believe it should just be driven from one single direction. If for some reason your designs are not being received so well by the market, that could cause the collapse of the company.

MF: Do you use your role as art director to commission other designers?

LN: Yes, but I first commission the other designers, and then I work as an art director to fill out what is missing. It's inverted; it is not that I am designing first and then calling on someone else to do the collateral stuff. It's very demanding in a way and can be very complicated to deal with so many different contributors, but it's also very satisfying when you see the work you're doing as an 'orchestra director' is translating into great results from your 'musicians'. I prefer to involve other studios as my musicians, and then my studio doesn't become crazy trying to manage everything.

I don't think art direction is forever. I think three to five years is about right – in that time, you can set a new trajectory, establish a way to work, introduce the company to different ideas and people, and then hopefully they start to walk that walk by themselves. Or maybe they choose to hire another art director.

MF: You've managed to diversify your income sources, which has given you greater stability, but, like any business, your work is subject to market forces and there is still variability – clients come and go, new opportunities come and go …

LN: Yes, and then you need to understand your capabilities and what you can and cannot achieve. If many opportunities come to you, you have to consider how many extra people you will need to service those opportunities. Do I want to hire more people in order to accept these new jobs, or do I prefer to maintain a team of a certain size and achieve a balance that feels manageable and gives me the freedom to say no? That is an entrepreneurial risk that every designer needs to be aware of. The success of a designer is a combination of numbers and creativity.

MF: Often when I talk to designers, there is a disparity between reputational success and financial success, and these elements of their career sit on different timelines and have varying levels of momentum. Have you been through the same?

LN: I often say that running a design studio is like running a start-up over ten years. You need to survive the first ten years and then you start to see some results. The royalties need to accumulate, your reputation and the quality of your work need to build up, and it all happens layer by layer and at different speeds. For example, you need to build twenty layers to be recognized, and then from that point there are another fifty layers to have some economic compensation for what you are doing. I don't think I've arrived there yet!

As an entrepreneur, when you can see that there is some financial structure, you need to invest in order to sculpt an even stronger direction that you hope will be understood by others. If you feel strongly about that direction, you have to keep persevering, navigate any criticism, and eventually other people will understand. It could take a few years, but if you take the direction that everyone else is going, it is too easy and too safe and there is the risk that you are just a follower.

When you have brands approaching you, it is always interesting to understand why they're approaching you. They immediately give you a perception of what you're doing, and then, when you see a pattern, you can ask yourself if that's how you want to be perceived and what you really want to do. It is an opportunity to find other tools to shift their understanding of what else you can do for them. It is important to take time to redefine what you're doing, work out the parts you enjoy and then find opportunities in those areas.

MF: We've talked about royalties and fees, but what about equity? Is that something you've negotiated before?

LN: Equity is interesting, because it's a way of making you feel more invested in the brand. However, equity is only toilet paper until you're ready to sell your shares. It's a start-up mindset, but I would prefer to own shares in a solid company. Quite often with a new start-up, they attract a lot of money from various investors and they spend a lot to build up a product portfolio that is then hyped up to boost their brand value and market visibility. This creates a kind of bubble that is fuelled by the creation of lots of products of questionable quality, and this kind of poisons the market. It is a different game.

Failing as a start-up is part of that game. I'm still Italian, and for me, bankruptcy is a failure. I don't want to be part of that game because I care too much about what I'm building up. In my opinion, to play that game you need to be detached from what you are doing. I'm not interested in building up something that I will sell in five years; I prefer to invest forty years of my life in it.

Sustainability, Values and Crisis

MF: 'Sustainability' is a word that is so used and abused these days. Within the context of materiality and three-dimensional design, what does sustainability mean to you?

LN: I think sustainability, especially in product design in general, of course must consider materials, production, life cycle, etc., but in reality, there must be proper infrastructural support that allows you to think and act in that way.

For example, with my client Offecct, I designed an acoustic panel called Notes; the core of the panels was filled with the discarded fabric offcuts from their upholstery department. The idea was to use a material that was considered garbage and, within the same company, create a new product that is filled with this unwanted material, and then covered up with a virgin fabric. Aesthetically, you could choose the fabric you want and then, at the end of the product's life, that fabric could be shredded and become part of the core of the next one … The idea was to close the material cycle.

The intention was principled, but the problem was that their use of fabric for upholstery was very efficient and they often didn't generate enough offcuts to fulfil demand. The next best thing was to try to find other companies that were discarding their fabric waste, and buy it from them. But in the end, it was not possible because there was no system or infrastructure in place to buy this kind of waste.

Frustratingly, the integrity of this approach failed because we didn't consider the amount of discards necessary to maintain this kind of idea. At the same time, it became clear to me that, in a country such as Sweden that is very focused on sustainability, there still wasn't a proper infrastructure to support this circular approach to materials.

The other difficulty to consider is that perhaps the processes involved in the recycling of materials are less sustainable than the production of the virgin material. So, I have asked myself many times, how can we try to be more sensible about these topics? In the end, after much frustration, I realized that the only way to be sustainable is to question what people really need.

We have to take a step back and think about the quality of the product itself. By using the skills of the human hand, I think we can produce a special design that resonates with people, that they will take care of and will want to keep. This achieves longevity for that product that is perhaps more sustainable over the years than a product that can be endlessly recycled.

MF: Yes, the longevity argument is that if you make something well in the first place, it is much less likely to end up in our recycling or waste streams.

LN: Yes. In design, longevity embraces lots of different topics, but principally it places a lot of importance on handcrafted work. Of course, the labour cost of handcrafted pieces is much higher than that of mass-produced. The real work for us is to re-educate the customer to understand the value of what they are paying for. In my opinion, that is what we should work on as designers.

More than ten years ago, I had a chat with the designer Enzo Mari, who was a sort of rebel and crazy theorist. I liked his point of view when he said that the responsibility of a designer is that you don't only consider the product that you are designing but also the opportunity to create jobs for people. Of course, their processes can also be poisoning our planet, so we need to find a balance between creating jobs and the extent to which we are poisoning our world to create those jobs.

MF: There is an element of privilege that comes with what you're saying; yes, we can try and convince people to buy into quality and longevity, but more often than not, these products come with a price tag that is hard for a lot of people to afford.

LN: I agree, but I'm not talking from an elitist position. In the past, if you wanted something special, you might say 'I can't afford that but I love it,' and you might save the money to eventually buy it and look after it. Alternatively, if the need was more urgent, you would search for the next best company that fit your budget. But then what happened was that the capitalist message told us to consume regularly according to every little whim. Functional needs were fulfilled easily and cheaply, and standards of quality and longevity were lost. Suddenly, we stripped away the value; we could treat objects badly, then just throw them away when they got damaged and replace them cheaply. This is crazy – we need to respect the objects that surround us, kids included!

For example, my mother still has the Coronado sofa designed by Afra and Tobia Scarpa for B&B Italia that she bought forty-five years ago, when I was born. It still has all the scratches that I left on that sofa, but it works perfectly and is even nicer with the patina of age. That is something I'm trying to think about when designing products – will it still look good when it's scratched and imperfect?

MF: Yes, and often natural materials are the most gracious in that respect, not the synthetic ones.

LN: Certainly plastic is spoken about as the devil [when it comes to] the environment. Plastic itself is not the problem in my opinion – it's how we use it. If you design a beautiful plastic chair, that product can be forever and perhaps has a longer life than a wooden chair. But it must be designed in a certain way, with a quality that enhances the material characteristics of plastic.

For me, it is all about attitude: attitude of consumption; attitude in understanding the value of things; attitude that when you are buying something you are not just buying an object but also a piece of culture that embodies a human skill.

How can we communicate more of that story? For example, I'm working on an exhibition, and next to every product that is included, I would like to include numbers that communicate how many hours it took to develop the product, how many people were involved, how many suppliers, etc. Then the amounts for each product would be added up and the total figure would become the title of the exhibition, nothing else. Perhaps there would be 3,500 people who worked for more than 100,000 hours! This would help people to understand that what they are buying is not just a functional object – they are buying many other things. But if you're not explaining that, of course, everything will just be judged by the price.

MF: Yes, and the same analogy can be applied to other areas of life, such as food – people don't place enough emphasis on how our food is grown.

LN: People don't understand the value of what they're buying. Fast fashion, for example – how is it possible to buy a T-shirt for €3? If you knew the polluting and exploitative conditions under which that T-shirt was made, you might think twice before buying it.

In my opinion, the first step to being sustainable is to encourage people to understand the value of things and what is behind them. From there, you can start to build up more infrastructure that is based on the sensibility of the people. For example, we could place more emphasis on the second-hand market and the restoration of products.

MF: Yes, we've certainly lost the culture of repair.

LN: Yes. Take a damaged sofa, for example – in the past, you could find someone local with the skills to repair or reupholster it. Now those skills are hard to find. We really need to push to sustain these skills as an important part of the sustainable toolkit.

MF: How do we encourage that side of society? It seems people don't want to get their hands dirty any more with that kind of hard work.

LN: That is the project we need to create! I don't think it's about pushing people to repair stuff by themselves. But we can help them to understand that if you increase the quality of how a product is made, there is less risk that you will need to repair it. We also need to make a better connection in our education; why, for example, does everyone need to work in the service industry? We need to converge again on some core skills.

MF: Earlier, you said that as a designer, you want to design things that people need. But that's a very subjective thing to say, because everyone has different needs. And, despite our multitude of differences, humans have already created so much of what we need. How do you temper that by adding new things to the world?

LN: I don't think the market needs a new chair or a new sofa or a new piano ... there's already too much available. I'm not thinking that I will change the world through my job. But for the niche of people who like what I'm doing, I want to offer them products that are not purely functional. It is my role to imbue each product with a cultural story linked to the people, the skills and the processes involved in its making. This all adds value.

MF: Do you think that with newer production technology and more sophisticated procurement processes, we will be able to lower our reliance on faraway factories, speculate less on production volumes and perhaps make things more locally and on demand?

LN: Yes, but again it comes back to the need to rebuild a lot of lost infrastructure. For example, take the UK – a lot of small and medium-sized industries [there] have disappeared. That was off the back of a political choice to move people into the service sectors. If we want to go back to a more sustainable way of producing, each country should rebuild its infrastructure to allow localized production. We need to revive a skilled workforce with that infrastructure.

MF: Let's talk about the multitude of materials that are available for you to work with. How much is it your responsibility to ensure that the materials you're specifying in your designs come from responsible supply chains that are not damaging the planet?

LN: There is a much more complex dialogue that you need to open up with the company you are working with to understand the entirety of their supply chain. A question I always ask is whether the company adheres to any certification schemes, which acts as a guarantee of traceability.

But thinking we can totally change the direction of a company with one project … I've tried but never succeeded. A company needs to be ready to support that kind of vision. The foundations of change need to be in place already, which becomes the basis for new designers to work on new projects to change the trajectory of that company completely. But that first requires a cultural shift to take place within the brand.

MF: What about governments and their policies? Won't legislation create the environment in which certain materials or processes are acceptable or not, or require certification or accreditation?

LN: Yes, there are some developments happening. For example, I believe in the USA there are now some certifications to assess the environmental impact of products and also furniture.

I think there should be a new course in design schools that matches design thinking with politics. Governments should be obliged to have designers to think about how we can be more creative in making the changes that need to happen. Designers would add a more holistic view that I don't think politicians have.

MF: What about a product's end of life? Very few brands pay any attention to what happens to a product once the warranty has expired. As much as you can design a product to have a long life, be repaired or handed down between generations, do you design for its eventual death? Design for disassembly, if you like.

LN: Yes, this is becoming more important. A complex interplay of materials makes it difficult to repair a product, but it also makes it expensive to disassemble. Take the LED bulb, hailed as an energy-efficient, eco-friendly alternative to the incandescent light bulb. There are claims that one bulb will last 25,000, 50,000 or even 100,000 hours. Yes, it consumes a lot less power across its long life. But a lot of light fittings now integrate LED bulbs that are not possible to remove and replace. That bulb may last several decades, but then what? Where will all these redundant fittings go? So often, we are thinking about rapid fixes in this period of emergency, but not about the long-term impact.

MF: Personally, I feel the design world is a bit stuck right now. Perhaps we need a movement?

LN: There is no dialogue and there is no support for dialogue any more. In the past, magazines created and supported a lot of dialogue. Criticism was more pronounced, people took a position and debates took place. But then it became dominated by advertising and design became more cosmetic and without a deeper purpose.

We need to put aside our egos and our judgement and try to see ourselves as part of a constellation, because without that joined-up discussion, we will not progress collectively. We need to work on opening up the dialogue in our community – not just showing new things but prioritizing a real dialogue so that we keep moving in a positive direction and don't become stuck.

MF: Do you think there's a loneliness in design, where there are too many individuals working alone on their own thing, too much emphasis on authorship and the protection of individual ideas and not enough emphasis on this idea of collaboration? Some problems are so complex that they demand collaboration.

LN: For a lot of us, there is less appetite for this because we're worried about keeping our businesses up and running and maintaining what we have, rather than looking at what we need. Also, as designers, we are all observing each other and most of the time criticizing others because they are doing something different from us. But there is no connection between us because most of us are focused on maintaining that tiny piece of the puzzle that we have been able to build up, but we are not able to influence the entire picture. I feel as though there is nobody at the cultural level who is really looking at the entire scenario and trying to analyse it properly.

MF: Maybe the sort of things we're discussing come about through crisis, when people are forced to come together through urgency.

LN: I'm not sure a huge crisis unifies everyone – people start to guard their own interests, as Daan Roosegaarde told me once. But when you look at our planet from space, it looks tiny and that's a reminder of how small we all are and how mad all our stupid conflicts and crises are. Astronauts often come back to Earth with a completely different perspective on who we really are in the scheme of the universe. It emphasizes how important it is that we all work towards the same goals if we are to survive for longer on this little blue planet.

MF: The optimist in me hopes that we will work together like that. But invariably human nature causes us to start fighting, and we want to be bigger or better or more powerful … we just can't help ourselves, it's a self-destructive attitude.

LN: Without knowing it, I think we are probably quite keen on our own extinction. We are too arrogant to change and sacrifice a few things. We often know that our actions are harmful, but at that moment in our lives it suits us and we make exceptions for ourselves. It's a sort of selfishness. And we are all selfish, some more than others. I think it's part of the nature of our species to walk into self-destruction, without even knowing it.

But right now, we think we will be here forever. We will not be here forever. It's kind of beautiful to think that, just as we are admiring the skeleton of a dinosaur in a museum today, there might be another species that will look at us in the same way in the future.

MF: Speaking of dinosaurs … I often feel younger design students look at our generation and think we're crazy for walking around big trade fairs getting excited about chairs. They're thinking we've got big problems to fix in the world and they're keen to work on system change to get there.

LN: In that sense, I feel my role is to be part of a big discussion and help, through my network, those who are studying design to think a little bit outside the box and eventually connect them with situations that can be useful for their purposes. For the evolution of the profession, it will be much more interesting for them to tackle topics where there is a real need. In that sense, we are dinosaurs – in fifty years, I don't know if designers will be doing what I'm doing right now. Hopefully not!

But also we need to consider that each of us makes up a little piece of the puzzle, and if we are able to be in connection with another piece of the puzzle that is doing something differently, and they are all connected in some way … then we can create a constellation that can become a movement. If there is a common ground that wants to have a proper impact on society, I think it is also the responsibility of each designer to be part of that. Individually, I don't think we can change enough.

Teaching the Young, Learning from the Young

MF: You've done some university teaching over the years, including at IUAV [Università Iuav di Venezia]. What are your observations of that new generation?

LN: What is clear is that all the students are very keen on sustainability – that is the first topic for every kind of project. Of course, they like the idea of designing a lamp, a chair or a sofa, but I encourage them not to start with such a defined idea but to take a holistic point of view about the products that we will need and we don't know it yet.

We recently did a project looking at the everyday rituals in our lives. I wanted to communicate to the students that they shouldn't just look at what a company is already doing – they should analyse our needs. Perhaps they start by understanding ancestral rituals and investigate how those have evolved over time. What could be the next step in that evolution? It was quite interesting to see the ideas that emerged.

MF: I feel as though the younger generation doesn't care so much about the ego trap of having their name all over the product.

LN: Yes, I think they deeply understand that it's no longer only about the single person, but more about the community. It is a generation that grew up surrounded by internet-enabled screens, which are isolating. I think they feel a kind of loneliness because so much of their contact with other people is through these devices. When they have the feeling that they can be part of a real community alongside other people, I think they embrace that collaboration. I think it's fantastic.

MF: If you were their age again, what would the younger Luca say to the Luca of today?

LN: The young Luca would say to the old Luca, just do what you are doing but always have fun. The young Luca was having a lot of fun when I was playing basketball, but then, as I got better at it and the game became too serious, I started struggling. When I had to train every day with a super-serious coach, it became less fun and felt like a job. I started to have a sort of nausea every time I saw a ball! So everything changed …

It is kind of the same story with design. I didn't start designing because I wanted to become a world-famous designer; that was not my goal. My passion was becoming my job and I was having fun with it. And then when you start to have more responsibility and you build up a structure and a studio and involve other people, everything becomes more serious because there is money involved, and other people's livelihoods. But I think the fun part is what makes the difference – it brings a lightness to be more naïve, in a good way.

MF: And what does today's Luca say to the young Luca?

LN: Always be curious, because that's what makes you think differently. Curiosity allows you to explore other territories without being dominated by the knowledge of your past experiences. If you look at the work of Eero Aarnio, he is a ninety-year-old designer in the middle of a forest in Finland and you get the feeling he is having fun. Despite his age, he probably has the imagination and curiosity of an eighteen-year-old. He has been able to maintain that pure aspect of creation.

MF: Depending on how long you choose to work in your life, you are currently about halfway through your working career. Where would you like the next twenty or thirty years to take you?

LN: I would love to achieve the freedom not to be worried about income, paying the bills and stuff like that. I would like to achieve a sort of status that allows me to only do things I really like to do. So, if I were to receive twenty proposals and none of them really inspired me, I could say no to them all. Instead, maybe that year I would dedicate to doing some research by myself.

MF: Now, let's fast-forward to thirty years from now, when you and I are sitting in the Bahamas with a cigar and a whisky, two old men reminiscing about our lives. We are looking out into the world and the world is shining back at us. What is the world that you would like to see?

LN: I would love to see a greater acceptance of diversity – diversity of people, diversity of ideas, diversity of opinion – so that there is an open debate about the things that are currently treated as taboo. I think when people start to talk openly about stuff, you start to digest more. And when you digest more, you don't judge the unknown as a risk to you. I think this could help to stabilize some of the tension that is felt in the world right now.

I would love to see less judgement about what is right, what is wrong, what is Western, what is Eastern, what is North, what is South … we need to try to respect the different cultures by developing a sort of education that helps us to think more openly and with tolerance. Of course, it's important to maintain our roots but also to accept the differences surrounding us.

Also – and maybe this is a little bit romantic – I would love to see more respect, especially for older people. I'm talking about respect in the sense of having the curiosity to listen to the experiences of an older person because that knowledge can make your life richer. I think we've lost quite a lot of that respect.

MF: And what if, as we were sitting in the Bahamas, the reality of the world was very different? What if the destruction from climate change was really crushing the world as we know it?

LN: A single designer working alone cannot solve those kinds of problems – we need to act as a community. I think designers would work on designing a plan more than designing individual items.

MF: It feels as though it is only when an acute crisis hits that humans are jolted into making changes.

LN: Design has become responsive, particularly in the past twenty years; if there is a demand, we respond to that. It is too expensive and risky to research a potential problem and develop a solution before the problem has hit us.

MF: Sure. But take a crisis such as World War II – almost overnight, entire populations were required to shift their focus completely in order to fulfil the complexity of tasks around fighting and survival.

LN: Yes, of course there was some intuition from the designers and entrepreneurs at that time that they had almost no choice other than to try and change their production to meet the needs of society at that moment. The challenge today is to pre-empt what the specific need will be.

I think probably the biggest needs for humanity right now are not objects. We need to have a clearer view that the way we are living now cannot be sustained in the future. So we need to switch, and we need to switch pretty quickly. I think within the next decade there will be a much clearer idea of the areas we need to focus on.

MF: We've spent all our time talking about design. On the assumption that you're maybe too old to take up professional basketball again, if you had to do something else completely, what would you do?

LN: I would open a restaurant. I think it involves a lot of things that are similar to being a designer: you serve people through the ritual of eating and socializing; you focus on quality because that plays into the experience; there is the opportunity to be innovative and daring with ingredients, evolving constantly with the seasons; you still have contact with other humans; and, as a chef, you can really push yourself to see what magic you can create. And crucially, I would have fun doing it.

074. Ethimo, Pluvia, 2017

Scattered on pavements or crowding piazzas, woven plastic chairs were an iconic element in Italy in the 1980s. For Pluvia, the new outdoor stackable chair designed for Ethimo, Luca Nichetto returned to that image, rethinking it in a contemporary version. Pluvia has an elegant structure made up of the rounded lines of the aluminium frame and the soft curves of the woven backrest in synthetic fibre. →

075. Fogia, Jord, 2017

The modular sofa system Jord marks the encounter between Italian and Swedish heritage in the quest for a perfect balance of proportions and materials. The name, meaning 'earth' in Swedish, emphasizes the low, wide structure of this piece, typical of the Italian tradition in sofas, while the sophisticated selection of material and colours reveals its Scandinavian roots. Adaptable to a variety of environments, Jord also adapts itself to the requirements of the user, enhancing comfort with collapsible arms and backrests. →

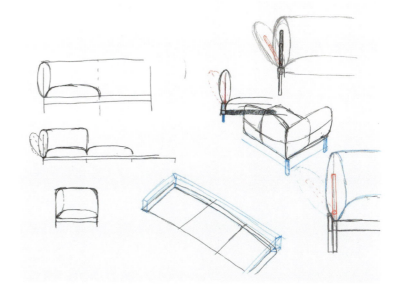

076. Fogia, Luft, 2017

Everything about the Luft vases is essential and organic to its concept, an homage to one of nature's four fundamental elements: air, the most intangible one. Its name is Swedish for 'air'. The natural yet supremely skilled action of the artisan glassblowers in Murano who create and shape it gives Luft its harmonious, rounded lines, which are inspired by hot-air balloons. Its colours, warm grey and dark amber, fade gradually to transparent at the top of each of the two sizes. →

077. Land Rover, Censer, 2017

The Censer scent diffuser, an exclusive accessory that was part of a Land Rover project for Paris Design Week 2017, takes cues for its distinctive design from the refined details of the new Range Rover Velar. Its 18-carat-gold-plated body, shaped through a 3D printing process, hides an Alumina ceramic core that absorbs the desired perfume and releases the aroma over time. The finishing touch is the hide lattice that complements Velar's sleek interior. →

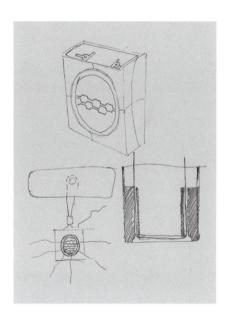

078. Moooi, Canal, 2017

During long summer days in Venice, sunlight shines on the canals and plays on the multicoloured bows of moored boats. Named after an iconic feature of the city, Canal preserves its Italian heritage in a contemporary product whose shape and colourful fabrics evoke those typical Venetian boats. Both the monochrome multi-tone look and the playful colour-combined version of the chair can be tailored through bespoke embroidery. →

079. &Tradition, Lato, 2018

The minimalist elegance of the Lato table echoes a playfulness inherent in the image of a caramelized apple or a lollipop. The marble base, while pursuing the inspirational aesthetic vision, also guarantees solid stability. It hides a steel core to which is anchored the slim tubular pole that connects the base to the top. Lato comes in different heights and dimensions, allowing it to be used as a side or coffee table and to adapt easily to different environments. →

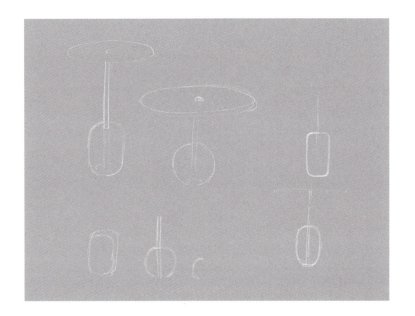

DESIGN IS A GOOD WAY TO GET IN TOUCH WITH OUR FELLOW WOMEN AND MEN

BEATRICE LEANZA IN CONVERSATION WITH FRANCESCA PICCHI

Design is a Good Way to Get in Touch with our Fellow Women and Men.
Beatrice Leanza in Conversation with
Francesca Picchi

Francesca Picchi: Before moving to Lisbon, where you're now the executive director of the Museum of Art, Architecture and Technology, you lived for seventeen years in Beijing and were the director of Beijing Design Week. It was natural for Luca Nichetto to meet you when he first went to China. He says you took him out of his comfort zone. How did your meeting come about?

Beatrice Leanza: Luca arrived in Beijing to present his first Chinese project during Beijing Design Week, an event involving designers and architects from around the world. He had just started working with some Chinese brands and it was his first time in China. We met largely by chance, as it happens. It's the way things come about at this type of event.

Beijing Design Week had been launched not long before, and I'd taken over as director less than two years after its foundation. What I wanted to do was not simply to copy the model of the design weeks in the West. Rather, I was interested in transforming the design-week paradigm into a more open formula, which could be developed as a great festival capable of establishing very rich, enduring ties with the city.

Beijing Design Week was a public project, promoted by the Beijing municipal government, the Ministry of Culture, the Ministry of Education and the Ministry of Science and Technology. So the project I developed sought to create networks of relationships that would continue to have a real impact on the city's everyday life in future years. At that time, our work was concentrated in the Dashilar quarter, a neighbourhood of hutongs [alleys] south of Tiananmen Square. It has passed through intense changes because of the many developments built in the twentieth century and particularly the new millennium. This is an extremely dense urban area, heavily populated, so our work attempted to network the potential, ideas and creativity bound up with the thinking of the designers to foster a type of long-term activity that would have a real power to affect these communities, which originally grew up as urban villages.

When I met Luca, I knew he was in town for other reasons, but I immediately plied him with questions: 'What can we do together? What are you doing for Design Week? Have you got anything we can include in the programme?' It was natural for me to show him around Dashilar. We went for some great walks in these wonderful corners of Beijing, inhabited by communities that it's not easy to form ties with, since they have their own way of life, with its patterns established over many years and notable for its social cohesion. So much so that part of our work, as a platform for Beijing Design Week, consisted of efforts at mediation that involved working closely with local associations.

These walks were the only way to understand such places, experiencing them from morning to evening, seeing how people used the streets, however narrow, which functioned rather like town squares, and the different ways the locals lived in the communal spaces. I suggested to Luca that he adopt a different approach in relating to life in China, and encouraged him to explore some of the inner workings of this world.

If he wanted to present his works at Design Week, it would be perfect, but if he was interested in forming closer ties with the local communities, being ready to get involved and question the strategic role of design in twenty-first-century megacities such as Beijing, perhaps he could do something different.

So what ensued was not a project that grew out of some preconceived commission. Rather, it arose from this type of conversation, of a kind I had with a lot of other designers. I think Luca was particularly struck by the community life, and perhaps he felt it resonated somehow with the place where he was born and grew up in Italy, the island of Murano in particular.

FP: It can be said that western people felt a profound curiosity about China in those years. More than ten years had passed since China joined the World Trade Organization in 2001, and it was in a phase of transition, the heart of a great transformation. Luca arrived in Beijing because he had built up contacts with Chinese companies in a rather unplanned way. He had made some acquaintances during the Salone del Mobile in Milan and they took him to Beijing for one of his first architecture projects, the showroom of a company that exported brands Luca worked for in Italy.

BL: The project that developed as part of Beijing Design Week also came about by chance. I met many people who were visiting China, but with Luca I started a conversation about what was happening. There was a lot of energy at the time.

Some of the younger entrepreneurs were starting to emerge, with a very keen flair for marketing and public relations. A class of young Chinese designers who had studied abroad and returned to China was also just emerging and putting forward new ideas about working in manufacturing and industrial know-how.

These fortuitous events, including the search for new relationships, gave rise to a lot of discussion. The mix of voices and complementary experiences, made up of fusions between design, art, architecture, cinema and digital experiments, created an intense conversation, and it was not difficult for Luca to become involved.

The project he did was included in the project called 'Dashilar Pilots', a container that brought together works on different scales, from architecture to infrastructural or urban planning projects, all within the framework of a redevelopment strategy for one of the most distinctive neighbourhoods of Beijing.

We can describe these projects as a sort of acupuncture treatment applied to the historic urban fabric. Luca adopted a gentle approach as a way of coming closer to the reality of life in the hutongs and taking part, albeit with a small gesture, in the more general plan for redeveloping the old city. His completely natural choice was to design an object that had its own formal identity and could function as an activator, meaning it could merge with the social fabric of these areas in a very low-key way, without looking like an object parachuted in from above or attracting attention to itself. Rather, it had the power to be part of the life of the community by solving a small problem and simply being useful.

With the help of a lad from Beijing, Luca designed and built some coloured concrete benches that were donated to the neighbourhood and that people could use as they saw fit. A spontaneous version of street furniture. In general terms, about forty were made.

These benches were used until they wore out. I think they were destroyed, not through vandalism, but just because of the intensive use people made of them. As I said, the project was conceived and built quite naturally. Luca, after a first visit, planned to return to Beijing regularly because he had other projects under way and was building the Tales Pavilion. He would stay for about a week on these occasions, and found time to carry out his project while he was there. Through a sculptor friend I put him in contact with a young businessman who had a factory of reproductions of Greek concrete statues. He visited it and together they agreed to set up this production of Luca's benches. Formally, Luca said he was inspired by observing how people behaved. Since there was no street furniture, he noticed that the locals would bring their chairs from home to sit on outdoors, or to use as stands for displaying goods while sitting on the ground. So he designed a bench with two thick legs and a very simple seat, shaped like a biscuit. Normally it could be used as a bench, but it could also be placed upside down. The legs were two rather thick cylinders and they offered space both for sitting on, like stools, and for displaying goods, turning the piece into a minimalist commercial space.

This was the basic idea, then people dreamed up all sorts of unpredictable ways of using them. In some cases they used the cylinders as flower vases. It was very interesting to see the hacks people invented. It's a pity no record of all this remains.

Beatrice Leanza is the executive director of the Museum of Art, Architecture and Technology (MAAT) in Lisbon. She began her career as a curator at China Art Archives and Warehouse in Beijing. During her seventeen years in Beijing, Beatrice was creative director of Beijing Design Week from 2012 to 2016 and chief curator of the research program Across Chinese Cities featured at the Venice Architecture Biennale. She is co-founder of B/Side Design, an organization that spearheaded the establishment of The Global School, the first independent institute for design and creative research in China. Over the years her projects have focused on research-led experimentalism with a pronounced interest in cultural strategies of social engagement, community building and place making.

080. Arflex, Tellin, 2018

The Tellin lounge chair has the elegant appearance of a welcoming, open seashell. Two 'valves' meet and merge by overlapping to compose the seat and backrest, an encounter that marks the juxtaposition of the different colours of the upholstery. The enveloping roundness and generous dimensions of the seat enhance comfort, while a tubular metal structure gives stability. Available in fabric or leather, Tellin offers a palette of colours that goes from contrasting combinations to tone-on-tone versions. →

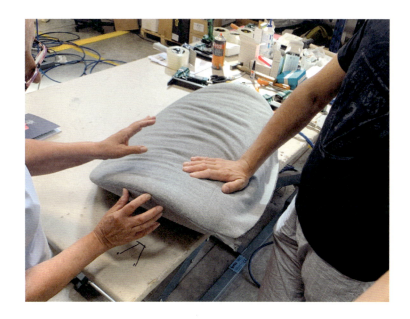

081. Coedition, Paris Showroom, 2018

Disengaging from a realistic and analytical approach, the showroom encourages a playful juxtaposition of colour with the hardness of materials, while shapes break the cement tones and the monolithic rigour of the facade. Elements in relief on the outer walls extend inside, becoming coloured figures that echo the letters of the word 'Coedition', visually dividing the environment into different areas. →

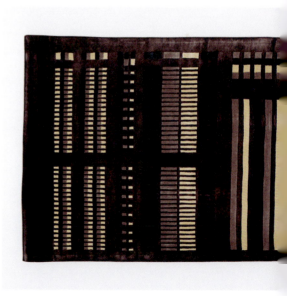

082. Fogia, Mame, 2018

Embodying a balance between classic and modern, the Mame bergère-style chair owes its elaborate simplicity to observation of the roundness and unbroken lines of the bean (or edamame) pod after which it is named. Its design aims to avoid having any building elements in sight, integrating part of the cushioning system into its body shell. The comfort guaranteed by the upholstered foam is enhanced by a companion ottoman, combining solidity and neatness in its metal structure while preserving balanced proportions. →

083. Fogia, Print Test, 2018

Despite its rich intricacy, the graphic pattern on the surface of the Print Test rug may look familiar. That is because it represents the lines and shapes of the standard print test. A dense, compact silk texture creates an embossed effect that adds tactility, while variations in sandy-scale and greyscale are available, along with multi-tone versions in which the elements of the pattern are gradients of the base colour. →

084. Hermès, Pure Imagination, Venice, 2018

A journey of memory through the toys, colours and textures of the childhood and an ode to the power of imagination. This window display in Venice is transformed into a box of multicoloured and multi-shaped elements, unique, with its own texture, shades and distinctive style. An inner richness and quality meets and mixes with Hermès products, giving rise to combinations that the imagination transforms into figures, places and situations of fantasy. (See page 83.)

085. Kristalia, Constellations, 2018

The design of the Constellations coffee table aims at the essential through the juxtaposition of shapes and materials. As a tribute to the professional and personal encounter between the sculptors Alexander Calder and Joan Miró, squares, partial ellipses and circles can be freely combined to create compositions of surfaces with various thicknesses and textures. Available in a variety of colours and materials, the tops sit on a metal structure of varying size, so discreet as to appear invisible, giving the effect of an abstraction of levitating objects. →

PROJECT 047
ZAOZUO COLLECTION

Project 047: ZaoZuo Collection

The year 2015 marked the time when China took centre stage in my professional life. Chinese design companies were increasingly seeking partnerships with Western designers when I received a LinkedIn message from Shu Wei, a Beijing-born entrepreneur who had studied overseas and worked in Silicon Valley but, nostalgic for her native land, returned to Beijing committed to launching a solo project that could be meaningful both for her and for the design milieu of her country.

In the wake of the growth of a lively and cool Chinese urban class, she envisioned the launch of an e-commerce site selling furniture. When Shu mentioned that consumer target, I immediately set off on a journey down memory lane, recalling my mother saving money to purchase B&B Italia's Coronado and the T69 dining table from Tecno: the appeal of home-grown design had skyrocketed in Italy in the aftermath of World War II, when the middle class grew in size and scope.

China is a land of possibilities, even if it can at times be bewildering for a European who doesn't speak the language. The communication gap made me feel lost in translation, and it took time to adjust to the faster pace of business and life. Nonetheless I accepted Shu's offer to become creative director for the brand, a role I held between 2015 and 2018. I had worked only in the premium segment of the market until then, so it sounded like a challenge that I was eager to embrace, and also an opportunity for a more meaningful design practice.

I encouraged collaborations with European and US designers, as well as spearheading the opening of the brand's first bricks-and-mortar store, in Beijing's Indigo lifestyle shopping mall. It all contributed to putting the company on the international design radar. The tie-up with ZaoZuo was not exempt from criticism, based on the assumption that I was betraying my native country, when in fact I pride myself on having safeguarded Italian design by helping a foreign company set up its own design lexicon and enter fair competition. For me it also served as a PhD in setting aside my hubris towards the team and learning from them the test-and-try approach, and their dynamism.

A turning point in the collaboration arrived when I realized I couldn't expect the same type of craftsmanship I was used to in Italy and Europe. They made me feel like an academic for the secrets and tricks I passed on to them.

This approach led to Silk, a family of monoshell chairs prototyped by my friend and master Luigi Cappellin. They were inspired by the Silk Road that had connected East and West for millennia, reinterpreting classic American designs from the 1950s through the lens of traditional Ming furniture.

Type: Art Direction, Furniture, Retail Design
Material: Various
Colour: Various
Team: Elsa Boch, Daniele Caldari, Francesco Dompieri, Alberta Pisoni
Time: 2015–2018
Client: ZaoZuo

086. Kristalia, Tenso, 2018

Echoing its name, what transpires from the Tenso sofa system is the intuition of an inner tension between its parts that keeps them firmly suspended and open, in the manner of a welcoming embrace. The slender lines and sartorial details emphasize the softness of the upholstery in fabric or leather. The modularity of the tubular structure adapts to different sizes of seating, while the backrest enhances comfort by incorporating an adjustable headrest. →

087. Matter Made, Legato, 2018

Like a musical score where every note is played in a smooth and connected manner, the Legato lighting system represents the stave where notes, in the shape of cones, are organized so as to compose different melodies. Each lamp is anchored to a rigid structure in aluminium made of several tiers, individual modules that allow different combinations. The bi-directionality of the light sources creates a play of reflections and shadows between the cones, emphasizing the volumes. →

088. Matter Made, Rotea, 2018–19

It is from the careful and precise spinning movement applied to the hot liquid glass that the Rotea collection of pendant lamps takes its name and features. *Roteare*, the Italian for 'twirling', is the technique used by master craftsmen in Murano to create the lamps' blown-glass covers. Apple-shaped as a tribute to the New York brand, the shades are available in four different versions, with thin white stripes on transparent or shaded globes and darker irregular stripes on white globes, highlighting the wisdom of the artisanal gesture through the uniqueness of each piece. →

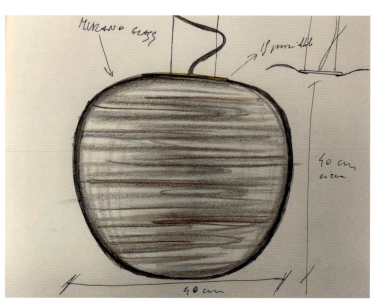

089. Moooi, Reflections, 2018

When the sun sparkles on the canals and filters through the stained glass adorning Venice's precious buildings, stepping into one of these structures means witnessing the spectacle of light creating its magic of abstractions. The Reflections rug reproduces on its surface a design made by photographing the overlapping of different glass reflections. The resultant varying scales, colours, textures and refractions inside the objects create elusive and ever-changing figures that are left for the imagination to interpret openly. →

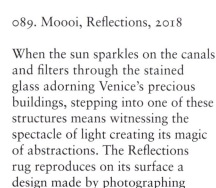

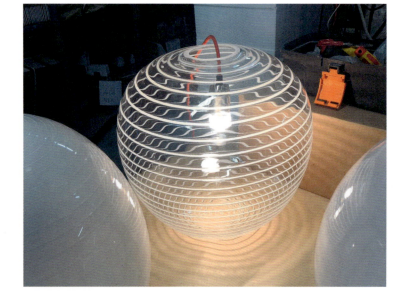

090. Offecct, Murano, 2018

To the austereness and elegance inherent in classical Scandinavian furniture design, the Murano armchair adds a modern touch by drawing lines that seem to evoke the fluidity and malleability of heat-treated glass. Like the tools shaping the hot glass, the seat and backrest are moulded by the structure, a minimal one in tubular metal defined by smooth curves ending in a small offset, which is useful as a handle or a hook for bags or coats. →

091. Parachilna, Gemo, 2018

Gèmo, 'yarn ball' in Venetian dialect, refers to the distinctive shape and texture of the mouth-blown glass lampshade. The streaks on its surface suggest the handicraft technique *molatura*, by which the artisans imprint engravings directly on the glass. The dimmable light emphasizes the intensity of the striped motif while the slim metal legs, available in black chrome and brushed brass, give Gemo stability and adaptability in its three versions, as a table, floor and ceiling lamp. →

PUSHING ACROSS BOUNDARIES

SHU WEI IN CONVERSATION WITH MAX FRASER

Pushing Across Boundaries.
Shu Wei in conversation with Max Fraser

Max Fraser: Tell me about your brand ZaoZuo, and how it started.

Shu Wei: The meaning of ZaoZuo is a combination of two Chinese characters: *zao* means 'manufacturer' and *zuo* means 'design works', and we are doing exactly those two things. We collaborate with global designers from China and overseas and we commission and produce original design works for the Chinese local market, especially for the younger, more energetic, urban middle-class users. Our main customer profile is female, 30–40, with a taste for the lifestyle we're offering and the economic means to buy it.

When we started this company in 2014, we wanted to create a one hundred per cent original design brand for young Chinese consumers. People thought we were crazy. But I think the future belongs to something more positive, and we want to make the changes as progress for society.

China has very mature supply chains and manufacturing industries, but the design industry is just beginning. Consumers are growing faster than the design industry, so it's the right time for our business. In order to achieve this, I told myself that I need to work with first-class designers, including Luca, as well as Richard Hutten, Roberto Palomba, nendo and many Chinese designers. We had this framework to utilise global design resources and combine with the Chinese manufacturing industry to create affordable but original design products.

We launched our first products in July 2015 with seven employees. We started online and then we opened showrooms in Beijing, Shanghai and Shenzhen in the second year. Now we have showrooms all over the country and we're also on the e-commerce platforms, so we are present on all the distribution channels. On the first day we launched, we had seven SKUs [stock-keeping units] on the website. In 2018 we had around 3,000 SKUs across 12 different categories, such as sofas, desks and cabinets, and then we expanded to textiles and lighting. By that point, we had become a lifestyle brand whereby you could decorate your home from one website. We realised we had too many products, so now we have 2,000 SKUs and around 200 employees.

MF: That's an amazingly fast trajectory of growth – is that because you didn't have much competition, as well as having access to a huge domestic market?

SW: Our speed of growth is not the fastest in China; we are actually quite slow because we're focused on making good products. Yes, the Chinese market is emerging really fast and it's not so crowded, but the competition here is fierce in terms of communication with customers, location of stores, etc., but not in terms of design. This is where we have an edge on the local markets.

MF: How did Luca come into the ZaoZuo mix?

SW: When I started the company, I wanted to work with the best designers in the world. So I started to research and created a list, and Luca was at the top of the list! I went to LinkedIn, sent him a message, explained my background and vision for the company, and told him I wanted to work with him. He replied positively and we started to work together before we met in person. And then, six months later, I went to Europe to meet him and talk about our first design. Things were very natural between us and we trust each other.

MF: Was it always your intention that Luca would be your art director and work on some of the other elements of your business?

SW: In the beginning, I didn't think that way. After working together for a couple of months, Luca had taught me a lot about the business and about how to shape ourselves in the industry. He's not a typical 'designer designer'; he also has the business perspective. I asked him to join the company as art director, and I also wanted him to be a partner in the company. He agreed and was thrilled to make things happen in the emerging market of China.

MF: You mentioned your mission to create products that improve the quality of life of the younger Chinese middle class. How have you seen that market change in the few years since you launched?

SW: I think it's changing very fast because of the economic situation. I was born in 1981, which was almost the beginning of a new age for China. In 1978 the country had started to embrace the world economically by opening factories, receiving investments and learning from the global market.

Things are changing every year. New consumers have emerged from a generation that uses the internet as an information window; they constantly see the best things in the world, they have learned what is beautiful and they have much wider eyes. My generation experienced the high speed of economic growth, which has now stabilized. Now the real-estate prices are very high, so the younger generation is quite financially sensitive. This means they want something beautiful and affordable. That is our mission; we want to create something really nice but not so flashy and not so luxurious – just really good daily design. I think our company has had an impact on the industry in China; many companies are following in our footsteps to create design brands, so the competition is much more than when we started.

MF: Your business is still relatively young. What are some of the challenges you've encountered over that period of time?

SW: Well, for an entrepreneur, ninety-nine per cent of the business is a challenge! Creating a design brand, the first thing is to control the supply chain. Because the factories don't belong to us, we've done a lot of work to control the quality and establish a good communication system with them. This is important because we produce so many products across thirty-seven different factories. That requires a lot of management effort, and we have a whole team dedicated to this; if there's one error, that can affect the whole system and create great delays with customer orders.

The second difficult part is around the key management. The retail business is all about people, about your sales teams, about how to inspire people, particularly if you're not directly in touch with the consumer.

MF: With regards to your factory partners, what has it been like to convey to them the brand messaging and all the standards that you want to achieve for ZaoZuo?

SW: It's been a huge challenge. We have our own inhouse research and development team, and all the technical parts are finished inhouse, not in the factory. We have a lot of quality-control engineers to work with designers and product managers and to deal directly with the factories. We also have a lab to work on the chemical and physical tests on all the products to ensure that the materials are environmentally friendly and pose no risk to human health. There are high costs to control the product quality, which means that our products are a little bit more expensive than the average price line of China, but the consumers trust us and they become loyal forever.

MF: What would you say you've learned from working with Luca?

SW: Oh, lots and lots! He acts as a kind of torch on the design industry. I have a good eye and good taste, but I'm more on the consumer side and he's more on the industry side, so we can work together to find the right design language and style for the consumer markets, and I will translate that for the Chinese market. We meet in the middle.

He also helps us to formulate the product strategy, which is not about single products but more about collections and making a correlation between many of the products that work together in the home.

Luca understands the industry side very well, and also the perspective of the other designers we work with. That means we can apply many of their techniques and skills to make the quality better and make better sense of the details. The Venice area (where Luca is from) has a long history of industry and they have lots of skills that we can learn and apply in China, paying attention to the small details and high standards. Luca has helped to push the company to the upper level.

An entrepreneur at heart, Shu Wei was running her own successful marketing and graphic design company before she had even completed her studies at Stanford University. In 2014 she founded ZaoZuo – a contemporary design brand focused on introducing affordable interior products to the young and increasingly affluent generation in China. She has worked with Luca Nichetto from the beginning, at first inviting him to design products for the brand before the relationship evolved and he became ZaoZuo's art director, working on a broader strategy with Shu.

 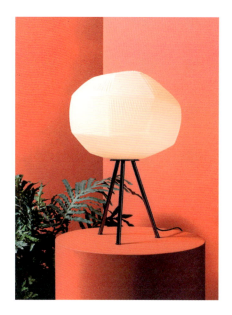

092. Stockholm Furniture & Light Fair, Ratatouille, 2018

A unique vision whereby the Design Bar and the Design & Architecture Talks meet for the first time. Like a Roman arena – a historic place for human rituals such as consuming food and watching shows – Ratatouille is an open, oval space, where symmetrical paths and functional areas echo French formal gardens, while a perimeter of monumental elements evokes the ruins of Stonehenge. →

093. Svenskt Tenn, Fusa, 2018

A personal interpretation of the Austrian/Swedish architect and designer Josef Frank's Terrazzo textile print, the pattern of which recalls the mosaics in old Venetian buildings, this collection of floor lamps, table lamps and candle-holders translates the design from fabrics to lighting. Handcrafted in Murano, Fusa takes its name from the Italian word for 'fused', evoking the special technique used to produce the distinctive colours and textures of the glass, all enlivened by the internal LED light that generates a play of refraction, opacity and transparency. →

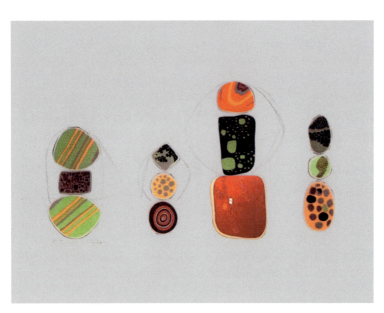

094. Svenskt Tenn, Heritage, 2018

In 1938 Estrid Ericson, the founder of Svenskt Tenn, held an exhibition featuring objects from Murano. Eighty years later, the *Heritage* exhibition again draws an ideal bridge between the small island in the Venetian lagoon and the city of Stockholm through a celebration of heritage. Within an environment inspired by the work of the prominent designer Josef Frank, Luca Nichetto's own upbringing in Murano and mastery of glass design and production shape an exhibition that highlights the quality of materials and the richness of different traditions of craftsmanship. →

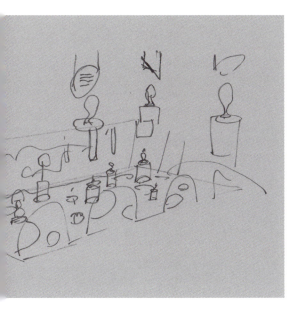

095. Tubes, Astro, 2018

Designed in the form of a small spaceship that is about to take off, the Astro fan heater can explore and land in various places within the home or office. To its primary heating function, it adds the technology of air purification, an option that can also operate in autonomous mode. There are touch buttons on the body whereby the user can activate the device and adjust its intensity, while a dedicated app can control it remotely through Bluetooth. →

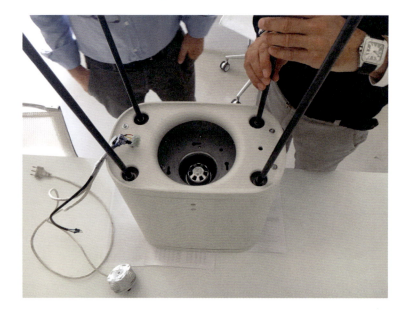

096. Sancal, Next Stop, 2018

The round parallelism of this volumetric sofa suggests comfort, while the collaboration with the textile designer Marie-Louise Rosholm introduces the innovation of a knitted textile as a joint between the parts. With its handmade pattern and gradient effect, the knitting technique avoids the need for stitching in the upholstery, a tailoring solution that guarantees its production to be a zero-waste process. (See page 65.)

PROJECT 038
NICHETTO = NENDO

Project 038: Nichetto = nendo

Some projects have no predetermined purpose, but stem purely from the human and professional desire to challenge oneself and the status quo or engage in a fruitful exchange. The collaborative venture with Oki Sato, founder of the design studio nendo, originated from these principles and turned out as a poetic dialogue between two designers of the same generation, two countries, two cities.

In 2013 the former editor in chief of *Form* magazine Hanna Nova Beatrice commissioned me to interview Oki for the magazine, during a trip to Tokyo that I had planned for the local design week. I had no journalistic background, and the prospect was both scary and intriguing. I met Oki for a coffee in Roppongi and the formal interview I had expected turned into an insightful and wide-ranging conversation that transcended my prepared questions to touch on such subjects as the collaborative approach between Shirō Kuramata and Ettore Sottsass, the history of design in 1980s Italy and Japan, and the two countries' different perceptions of colour. The two-hour conversation – which I recorded, and listen to quite often – ended on an upbeat note with a pledge to work together at some point.

Around Christmas that year, Oki came up with an idea about how to work together without the two of us being physically together. Inspired by traditional Japanese poets who used to compose collaborative poems, one writing down the incipit and the other completing it with the closing, Oki suggested that we emulate that process, ping-ponging sketches and ideas between the two countries.

The result was a widely stratified combination of our design practices, which also crumbled the widespread belief that designers are always competing against one another. By contrast, the Nichetto = nendo project is testament to the fact that a collaborative mindset is alive in the industry – despite having been dormant for some time – inspiring other designers and young talent to follow in our footsteps. The fact that some of the projects we developed were then produced was an unexpected and positive side effect.

Most importantly, the project spurred a real friendship that has stood the test of time. When I saw his design for the cauldron at the Tokyo 2020 Olympics, I felt proud for witnessing a great piece of design by Oki Sato under the spotlight of so many people.

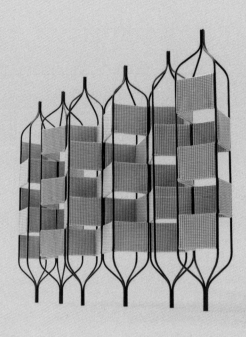

Collection: Nichetto = nendo
Material: Various
Dimensions: Various
Encounter: Oki Sato
Collaborator: nendo
Time: 2013

168.

097. Wendelbo, Floema, 2018

A family of tables whose minimalist design is characterized by the absence of edges, offering a welcoming elegance. The elliptical or circular roundness of the tops, which are available in stone or wood, is repeated in the curved details of the metal structure. In different heights and shapes, the versions of these tables offer a variety of surfaces to satisfy the different needs and uses in a working environment, from moments of focus to moments of relaxation. →

098. Wendelbo, Lilin, 2018

In a daily life in which we easily move through virtual and remote interaction, the Lilin sofa is conceived as an invitation to communication and conviviality. The soft shapes and rounded lines of the seat and backrest suggest a welcoming comfort, while the curve of the structure places those who sit on it in a more informal position, fostering relaxed communication. Lilin is a versatile solution whose bold design allows it to reinvent the space by undermining the orthogonal rigour of the environment. →

099. Bernhardt Design, Luca Collection, 2019

With a design conceived to enhance versatility while suggesting the comfort of the home space through the roundness of its lines, the Luca Collection introduces a flexible constellation of elements that are able to cover wide areas through the richness of their combinations, while also standing solo. Four universal structures form the foundation of the modular sofa system, allowing endless configurations through a range of backrests, seamlessly designed to be anchored to the base. →

100. De La Espada, Belle Reeve, 2019

Named in tribute to a significant place in the film *A Streetcar Named Desire* (1951), Belle Reeve is a sofa system characterized by the use and processing of a natural material, wood. The body made entirely of wood echoes the craftsmanship inherent in its construction, which is particularly visible on the side panels, whose texture gives lightness and dynamism to the structure. The addition of armrests and table surfaces breaks the symmetry and offers a choice of options and configurations. →

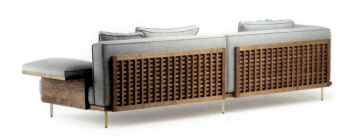

171.

101. Hermès, The Dream Carousel, Hong Kong, 2019

Questioning perception and imagination, this Murano-glass installation for six windows of Hermès' landmark Prince's store in Hong Kong combines the objects and oddities of a dreamworld. In a world of whimsy and lightness, lollipops showcase human features in a wild dance, and a fisherman welcomes his catch surrounded by oversized bobber floats and UFOs. Sweets explode into fireworks, disrupting the stillness of a nearby scene where fish swim among jellyfish and hot-air balloons. →

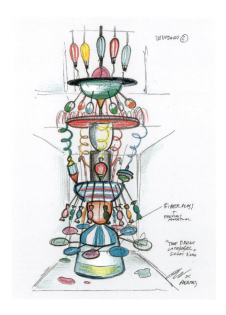

DIALOGUE, COLLABORATION AND LAUGHTER

OKI SATO IN CONVERSATION WITH MAX FRASER

Dialogue, Collaboration and Laughter.
Oki Sato in conversation with Max Fraser

Max Fraser: When and where did you and Luca first meet?

Oki Sato: I was first asked for an interview by Luca while he was in Japan for Tokyo Design Week in 2012. I remember clearly the day when I visited the meeting place, wondering if it was some kind of bad Italian joke, since I had never heard of being interviewed by a designer. Although I was well aware of his achievements as someone of my generation, I had no acquaintance with him. Perhaps it was because of his gigantic figure and tough appearance that my first impression was rather fearful, that I was going to be involved in some kind of incident, not an interview. But not long after our conversation started, I realized that we were interviewing for a Swedish design magazine. As a matter of fact, we had a lot in common in our approach and thinking about design, which made it easy for us to open up to each other. We ended up enjoying a conversation in the café for more than three hours, well beyond what we had originally planned, although it may have been a little annoying for the café! Since then, Luca is still the only person I can call a friend in the industry, even after more than ten years, and this was truly a fateful and precious encounter.

MF: In 2013 you both decided to collaborate on a small collection of products. Can you explain how that collaboration started and evolved?

OS: As I recall, the conversation naturally arose when we first met in Tokyo that it would be interesting to stage an exhibition together some day. The idea at the time was that we would bring each other's works and curate them together. However, when we met again six months later, we decided that it would be more challenging and interesting to create some objects together from scratch. Thinking that it would be better to have some kind of rules for this, we decided to adopt the traditional Japanese collaborative poetry method called *renga* (linked verse).

For some of the items in the collection, I came up with the initial concept and handed it over to Luca to flesh out the idea and give it shape; and for the rest of the items, we switched positions and went through the same process. We exchanged sketches via email, then met in person for discussions at events we were both attending, including the London Design Festival in September, the Maison&Objet trade fair in Paris in January, and the Stockholm Furniture and Light Fair in February. There was a time when we came up with an unexpected design for a new item in just fifteen minutes during a conversation in a café. It was almost like a jam session, where we were both drawing sketches at random, and as one of us showed interest in the other person's design, a new design would grow out of it.

MF: What was it that attracted you to work with Luca? You are based in Tokyo – what would you say are the cultural similarities and differences involved in working with a European designer?

OS: I feel that the many similarities and complete opposites between the two of us have both attracted each other. The similarities made communication and the design process run more smoothly, while the differences created unexpected chemical reactions.

One of the things we had in common was that we were the first generation of designers to emerge from an environment where the design industry had become unprecedentedly open and borderless through the rise of online design media such as *Dezeen* and *Designboom*, which proactively showcased young, unknown designers. We also share the flexible nature of thinking lightly, actively adopting new technology, enjoying dialogue with clients and collaboration with other creators, and embracing the flow of social change rather than resisting it.

The difference [between us] is that I am from Canada and currently working in Tokyo, with [an] architectural background, while Luca is a designer from Venice currently working in Stockholm, and is well versed in the ancient craftsmanship of Italy. Our different backgrounds were reflected in our collaboration, where each sensor was always running at the same time, with different detection capabilities, allowing us to always see several new possibilities for a single idea.

MF: Your collaboration was self-initiated and without the demands of a client. What did you learn from the process of collaborating with another designer?

OS: It was significant that the project was not commissioned by a client. By maximizing the use of mutual experience and knowledge, we were able to select the most suitable technology and materials for each idea. For example, for a fabric, Luca would talk to a Dutch manufacturer whom he knows well, while for that lampshade, I would approach a Japanese washi paper artisan who can do three-dimensional moulding, and so on. Luca's great network and versatility really amazed me during this phase, because these abilities can only be acquired by experiencing a large number of projects. He might say, 'If Company A can't do it, we ask Company B. If Company B can't do it, then changing the details opens up more possibilities.' His flexible ability to achieve something is significant. I think that is one of the reasons so many clients trust him.

Having the two design firms collaborate was also a valuable asset for nendo. Through not only the production phase, but also the collaboration of the two firms in taking photos in the studio, editing and creating the catalogue, setting up the exhibition venue, managing the day of the exhibition and handling interviews, my staff learned that what they had taken for granted was not always the right answer, given the differences in the way we approach our work and the issues we focus on. It was an unusual process in that each item was commissioned to be commercialized by a different manufacturer after the exhibition, which provided me with an opportunity to question the relationship between designers and manufacturers.

MF: In 2050, when you and Luca will be old men, how do you imagine the world will differ from today?

OS: However the world may change in the future, I hope Luca will continue to produce designs that will regularly make me jealous, and I look forward to collaborating with him again with a good laugh, just like last time.

Oki Sato spent the first decade of his life in rural Canada before moving to Tokyo, where he has lived ever since. Trained in architecture, he set up his design studio, nendo, in 2002 and has undertaken a vast array of products, buildings, interiors and exhibitions across the world. In 2005 his European studio opened in Milan, shortening the distance from his European clients. Oki's work often marries minimal form with accents of humour, imbuing every project with a friendly and approachable characteristic that has won him praise across the world. Luca Nichetto and Oki first met in 2012, and shortly afterwards their first collaboration was revealed.

102. La Manufacture, Luizet, 2019

As in a game that frees the imagination, Luizet is a modular sofa system that invites the combination of various elements through a distinctive geometry. An arched angular piece, a central square and a circular one, available both as a table and as a pouf, are the foundation for a variety of settings. Supported by a discreet, elegant metal frame, the three modules can be juxtaposed and mixed with the addition of cylindrical and rectangular cushions for the backrest. →

103. La Manufacture, Melitea, 2019

Through the juxtaposition of industrial materials and special attention to comfort, the Melitea lounge chair aims to present itself as a new classic. A linear metal structure, running from the legs up to support the back, is a distinctive element of the design. Two enveloping shells for the seat and the backrest create a timeless elegance, while their pattern of circular holes adds a modern architectural flair, functioning also as a grid to which to attach additional padding. →

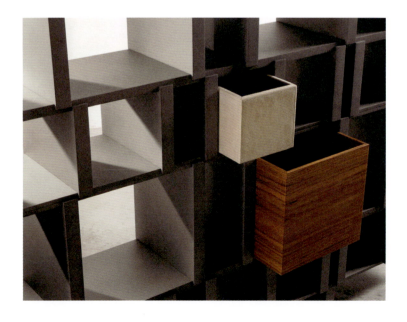

104. La Manufacture, Olindias, 2019

Characterized by curved lines and a contemporary elegance, Olindias renews the archetype of the bar stool, imbuing a classic piece with strong personality. A minimalist structure composed of tubular legs in metal converges towards the top to support the seat, the comfort of which can be enhanced with optional padding. As a constructional smart solution, the lower part of the legs can be unscrewed and replaced with pieces of different lengths. →

105. La Manufacture, Pyrite, 2019

Inspired by optical illusion artworks, the design of the Pyrite bookshelf amazes through an unexpected distribution between empty and full spaces and a structure in which horizontal and vertical seem to be reversed. The thin lines of the frame aim for invisibility while contrasting with the thicker dividers, in an unusual combination of widths. The different sizes and shapes of the sections combine to give a sense of movement, while panels in leather or wood can be added to the bookshelf. Pyrite can be used as a single module or as a bookshelf system. →

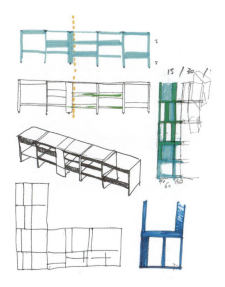

106. La Manufacture, Showroom, 2019

Through a minimalist approach and great attention to detail, this showroom in the heart of Paris invites the user to fully experience an environment conceived as a concept store. Visitors are welcomed into an open space characterized by a diversity of materials and textures and enlivened by their interaction with light, where each element has been specifically designed and manufactured, embodying a precious and eclectic combination of French elegance with the concept of 'Made in Italy'. →

107. La Manufacture, Soufflé, 2019

With a playful design and inflated appearance, the name of the Soufflé mirror borrows the French expression for 'blown', emphasizing its most evident and distinctive feature. A frame with the puffy, light appearance of a balloon hides inside a wooden structure and contains the arch-shaped surface of the full-length mirror. The tubular fixture allows a variable support point, both on the wall and on the ground, meaning the mirror can assume the ideal position for its setting. →

PROJECT 033
CASSINA
LA MISE

Project 033: Cassina, La Mise

To recite an old adage: when the going gets tough, the tough get going. This could be a tagline for my collaboration with the legendary design firm Cassina, the epitome of Italian design with more than ninety years of history, when they approached me for a competition against three other design studios.

I was in Paris in May 2011, a turning point for my career as I was 'graduating' from junior to senior designer. Upon receiving a call from Roberto Paiano, Cassina's design marketing manager, I initially thought he wanted to place the brand's furniture in my interior-design projects. On the contrary, and to my surprise, he was proposing that I enter a competition to become the design firm's next collaboration, following internationally acclaimed designers and legends such as Gio Ponti and Mario Bellini, just to name a few.

The competition's brief asked each studio to develop a new sofa concept based on the inner metal structure of Vico Magistretti's Maralunga design, which had been a Cassina icon of the 1970s, winning the Compasso d'Oro prize in 1979. Back in my studio in Porto Marghera, Venice, I addressed my team, explained the brief and bluntly said that I wanted to take part and win.

When creating La Mise (2012), the family of one-, two- and three-seat sofas that would be produced by Cassina, I was inspired by textile design, particularly the way kimonos are wrapped around the body. Translating this approach into furniture design, I envisioned a fabric to be folded to include the cushions and adjusted around the metal framework like a tailor-made dress. The technique also granted the object an empathetic quality, in that it reacted and adjusted according to its users.

My studio team and I developed several scale models to be presented to Roberto, Ferdinando Mussi (head of Cassina's R&D department) and Gianluca Armento, the brand's director at that time. During the presentation their eyes blinked several times, and their expressions were stunned, so I knew I had convinced them. It marked a moment of relief because, as much as the prospect of a collaboration inflated my ego, I was first and foremost committed to delivering a project that would satisfy both parties.

The work process that followed would teach me more than I could have expected. Not only did the Cassina team want the first prototypes to reflect the quality of execution that they had found in the scale models, but also they kept painstakingly fine-tuning the final objects, in a quest to reach design balance and perfection.

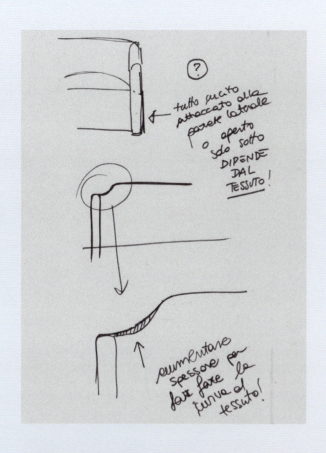

Type: Two-seater Sofa, Three-seater Sofa, Armchair
Material: Metal, Elastic Belts, CFC-free Polyurethane Foam, Feather Padding, Fabric, Leather
Colour: Various
Team: Francesco Dompieri, Alberta Pisoni
Time: 2012
Client: Cassina

108. La Manufacture, Tima, 2019

In the roundness of their sinuous bodies and their surprising transparency, jellyfish illuminate the darkness of the seas as dreamlike creatures. As though floating in the air, with light passing through the surface waves, bubbles and watery distortions shaped by master craftspeople, the Tima pendant lamp recalls that natural spectacle in the apparent lightness of precious Murano glass. Blooming from the centre, the light highlights the different finishes of its three sections. →

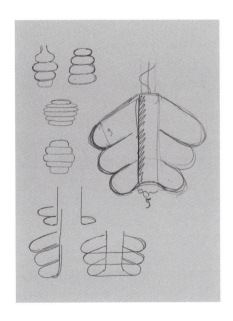

109. Monitillo Marmi, Nessie, 2019

Like a surprising but familiar presence, the marble Nessie doorstop embodies in its playful design the features of the famous Scottish lake monster. A handle in the shape of a head stretches out over a marble body as if emerging from the waters of Loch Ness, an effect that is suggested and highlighted by the difference of material and texture between 'neck' and 'body'. The handle is anchored solidly to the base, to which a metal plate with a felt surface underneath guarantees stability. →

110. Skultuna, Streamers, 2019–20

The Streamers candle-holder transfers to its design all the fascination brought back from a trip around Mexico, the volumes and the sense of grace over the unexpected yet solid equilibrium of Latin America's Modernist architecture. It consists of a series of geometric objects combined in different variations or fixed combinations. Candles stand still as though playing with the balance inside the variously shaped holders, never centred over their base, and the use of brass, silver, marble and stone creates a conversation between elegant materials. →

111. Wittmann, Nichetto Workshop, 2019–20

Rooted in the Viennese tradition of elegance and sophistication, as a bold reinterpretation of classicism while pursuing a sense of lightness and warmth, this universe of armchairs, lounge chairs, high-backed chairs, poufs and low and side tables gravitates around the sofa system, the core of the collection. It is an eclectic collection that offers endless possibilities for creating different settings and satisfying the most diverse needs. →

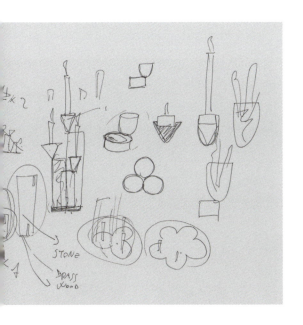

112. Lodes, Easy Peasy, 2020

With a sculptural design that aims for minimalist elegance through rounded shapes, the Easy Peasy portable lamp is composed of two elements. The body, consisting of a metal base containing a LED source and a white diffuser, is wrapped by one of two different glass bells that filter the light. A knob on top of the structure functions as a dimmer. Rechargeable and available in various colour combinations, Easy Peasy adds warmth and character to any environment. →

DESIGN IS ALL ABOUT PROPORTIONS

FERDINANDO MUSSI IN CONVERSATION WITH FRANCESCA PICCHI

Design is All About Proportions.
Ferdinando Mussi in conversation with
Francesca Picchi

Francesca Picchi: I see working for Cassina as a goal for a designer, but also a challenge. It means being welcomed into a community with its own rules and modes of expression. When Luca Nichetto arrived, you were in charge of the Research and Development Centre, and together, within a couple of years, you developed various projects: a sofa, a chair and a family of coffee tables. Can you tell us about the work you did together?

Ferdinando Mussi: We met at Cassina in 2012. Luca was very young and this was reflected in the way he approached products. It was very fresh and simple, a really direct approach. The brief we were given was to reinterpret the classic type of sofa, and we clicked right away.

From experience I knew that when you design a classic sofa you're a bit restricted. You have to keep to the fixed dimensions, proportions, measurements and reference points present in the products already made by the company.

It's well known that Cassina has a strong tradition of producing upholstered furniture, and this fund of knowledge is naturally passed on to the designers. But there's another important factor, perhaps one that is more difficult to decipher, and that's the ability to bring the designer into sync with the character of the company. Since Cassina has an important history, there are many details that, taken all together, define the character of a Cassina sofa. If you ask me to sum them up, I could mention the industrial conception of the frames padded with foam in a single piece, the almost obsessive research into the production of the cushions to ensure comfort, and the refinement of the stitching and the details finished with an artisanal sensibility.

FP: Each new sofa would be rather like a new individual in the evolution of a species, in the sense that Luca's sofa would have been added to a catalogue where the bestsellers and icons already stood out clearly.

FM: When Luca was asked to design a 'classic sofa', it meant a design capable of matching the traditional models of the armchair plus two-seater and three-seater sofa. As a young designer, he was expected to be able to bring new lustre to this clearly defined form, and he was good at giving it fresh expression while developing the well-established formula. He was very intuitive.

FP: I believe it involved designing a family of products rather than a single object.

FM: A family with details that would make all its components recognizable. In addition to the aesthetic qualities, you have to work to ensure comfort, and in general there are a lot more constraints than you can imagine. But design is all about the proportions.

Luca had the insight to treat the upholstery as if he were a tailor designing a bespoke suit, from the cutting to the seams, the padding and the folds. He also calculated the pleats at the point where the backrest turns into the armrests to smooth this transition and make the shape more enveloping. In short, Luca designed a single large garment that covers the back, armrests and seat, all sewn in one piece like a huge kimono.

FP: The sofa is one of those classes of objects that Italian designers have completely redesigned since the war, to the point where today it's common to speak of an Italian-style sofa. And it makes sense to say that the credit goes to Cesare Cassina and Piero Busnelli for inventing the type of sofa we know today. Now you've worked for both of them, what would you say?

FM: I can only agree: Cassina and Busnelli invented the contemporary sofa. In 1966 they created C&B (pairing their initials). With it they were the first to realize the importance of padding sofas with an innovative material such as polyurethane. B&B came later, when they split, and still has a very advanced foaming system that has been used to foam sofas in one piece by using moulds up to 2.4 m long!

I was lucky enough to work for B&B when Piero Busnelli, the founder, was still at the company, and I often heard him tell the story of his visit to the London Plastics Fair, when for the first time he saw polyurethane foam being moulded to make toys in the form of ducks. He remembered getting the idea at that precise moment to exploit the technology to produce upholstery. In fact, it revolutionized production, changing the history of the sofa.

FP: But when Luca joined Cassina, the pioneering season was over. On the one hand things would have been easier, because he could draw on the best that can be imagined in terms of know-how and experience in this field. On the other, I think, he had the problem of having to measure himself against the masters.

FM: Arriving in 2012 and measuring up to this tradition was not easy, but Luca certainly never lets himself feel daunted. After the sofa, we worked on the set of nesting tables conceived as tops suspended off the floor with a very lightweight structure. The tables, called Torei [2012], had tops of different shapes and heights and could be composed to form endless different combinations.

Later we tackled a more ambitious project: creating a chair with a purely industrial logic. It was a felt shell that came out of the mould without any need for further finishing. Luca encouraged us to experiment with a new moulding technique used only in carmaking to produce components for vehicle interiors, such as parcel shelves, roofs and door panels. It was a real production challenge to develop this chair, called Motek [2013], and at the Research Centre we put a lot of passion into it.

Luca had identified a firm that produced pre-impregnated laminated car components with a felt finish. We started talking to them about moulding a chair. Luca did a drawing and, on the basis of this, we began to study the mould. The difficulty was that both sides of the body had to come out perfectly finished from the mould, and it had never been done. It was a smart product.

Although it didn't stay in the catalogue long, the project helped us discover new production techniques with companies outside our sector, using a technology that had never been tested for furniture before. It was in keeping with the tradition and history of the Research Centre. Research, experimenting with new materials, has always been a part of Cassina's mindset, and its Research Centre was set up with just this mission. Think of Gaetano Pesce's research in the 1980s into coloured resins cold-cast in moulds, leading to the creation of the Sansone tables, or the experiments with felted wool treated with synthetic resins to make it structural that made it possible to produce the Feltri armchairs.

The Centre has an important history, but when Luca arrived, there wasn't the same investment available for experiments as before, when three per cent of turnover used to be reinvested in R&D. Management only wanted to support successful products.

FP: So is there a recipe for a successful product?

FM: Who isn't convinced they're onto a 'winning product' when they start a new project? As I said, I spent twenty-five years working with Piero Busnelli, who was a truly brilliant entrepreneur. He used to say, 'If we're smart enough to crack it three projects out of five, it will be an incredible breakthrough in quality!'

Ferdinando Mussi joined the Cassina Research Centre after working for two of the most renowned design companies in Brianza (the region around Milan), Tecno and B&B. Those unfamiliar with Italian product design may not realize just how much Brianza has contributed to its development and Cesare Cassina, from a family of traditional Brianza cabinetmakers, was the first to set his sights on modernity. He realized it could be attained only with the help of architects and designers, so he formed a series of successful partnerships with them. This story is part of Cassina's heritage, having become a sort of local legend, which everyone working in the furniture sector knows and draws inspiration from. They include Ferdinando Mussi, who has long been involved in research and development for the furniture business and has acquired great expertise in it.

113. Arflex, Supplì, 2020

Extending the softness and elegance within its perfectly balanced nature, the invitingly soft and sinuous curves of Supplì club chair exude warmth and embody a near-perfect spatial anchor for rest and relaxation. Its plushness is supported by slender metal legs, and the body is a simple integrated form enhanced by contemporary texture and fabric options. All the elements combine in an iconic, timeless object. →

114. DND, Viva, 2020

In continuous transition between immobility and mutability, the Viva door handle merges this contrast in a design that aims at ergonomics and visual sobriety. Characterized by a shifting appearance, the linear shape of the front view becomes surprisingly soft and sinuous depending on the point of observation. To the touch, the handle offers a sensation of strength and consistency enhanced by the hot-stamped brass, a material that guarantees solidity while remaining elegant. →

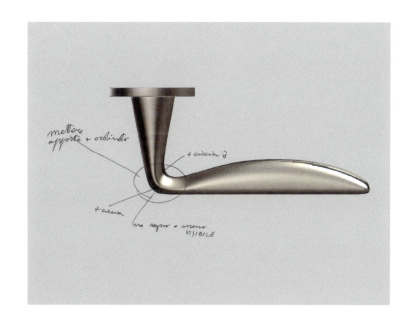

115. Et al., Classy Collection, 2020

Through exceptional attention to detail and a refined design, the Classy collection of chairs finds a natural balance between functionality and elegance. All the elements – chair, armchair and stool – find their signature mark in the shell, which, although sturdy, appears effortlessly moulded through simply being folded in two. The juxtaposition of different surfaces, matte below and shiny above on the ample seat and vice versa on the enveloping backrest, creates a play of contrast and increases the demarcation between the parts. →

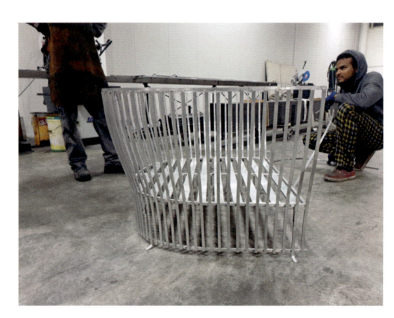

116. Ethimo, Venexia, 2020

The elegance of the urban furniture of the late nineteenth century lives again in a project that combines timeless charm and modern functionality. An aluminium structure recalling antique rails characterizes the sofas and the armchair, enveloping the generous, rounded forms of the seat with a feeling of simultaneous lightness and robustness. The padding in the large, soft cushions is made from recycled materials and completely waterproof, and they are upholstered in exceptionally soft outdoor fabric. →

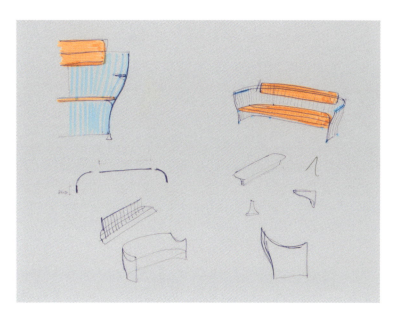

117. Gandía Blasco, Onde, 2020

Outdoor areas have become the setting for a variety of activities throughout the year, from retreats for a moment of relaxation to private temporary offices for remote working or shared workspaces. Onde is a collection of outdoor furniture that addresses this wide variety of needs through an endearing geometric design that balances versatility and comfort. →

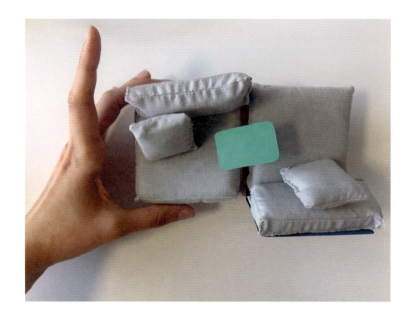

PROJECT 028
FOSCARINI
PLASS

Project 028: Foscarini, Plass

There are several layers to be considered in my collaboration with Foscarini, a company in the highest echelons of lighting design. It is without a doubt the design firm I owe the most to.

My bond with the firm dates from 1999, when, in my final years as an industrial-design student at Venice's architecture university IUAV, I interned briefly at the company, mastering mass production and prototyping. That year marked not only the beginning of my career but also a pivotal time for Foscarini, which was moving its headquarters away from the island of Murano to the mainland, and also progressively dismantling the production of Murano's mouth-blown glass lighting. Around the turn of the millennium, Marc Sadler designed for the brand a series of lamps called Mite and Tite, made of glass, carbon and Kevlar fibres, signalling a new experimental and transformative direction for Foscarini.

After my internship I proposed that the company's owners, Carlo Urbinati and my uncle Alessandro 'Sandro' Vecchiato, acquire some designs I had made with my fellow IUAV student and great friend Gianpietro Gai, with whom I also shared a consultancy role at the company in the material innovation and product development department until 2003. That year one of our co-designed lamps was produced under the name O-Space and soon acquired iconic status for the company.

My liaison with Foscarini has continued, leading to several projects. Arguably one of the most notable is the Plass pendant lamp of 2011, which was conceived to breathe new life into the artisanal glassmaking past of Murano.

Suppliers are often a hotbed of innovation, igniting designers like myself to think outside the box. Thanks to one of them I came across a unique rotational-moulding technique that transformed polycarbonate into transparent objects boasting the natural flaws and irregularities seen in handmade glass. However, it did not appeal to furniture clients, the supplier said, for its rarefied reflection of light and its imperfect surface.

Letting my whirlwind design thinking settle, I realized that size was what set glass and polycarbonate objects apart, since artisans cannot mouth-blow humongous items. The different discoveries – including research into materials, which has become integral to my design practice – came full circle. The giant pendant lamp that resulted reinterpreted the tradition of Murano glassmaking in the light of new processes and materials. Its polished pearl shape was rendered in a colour palette that nodded to traditional Murano glass nuances such as aquamarine blue and smoke grey. I named it Plass, a portmanteau of glass and plastic, the two materials that had seduced and inspired me the most for this project.

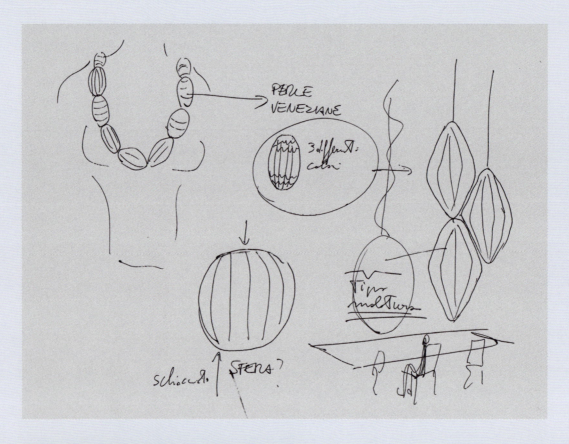

Type: Pendant and Table Lamp
Family: Plass
Material: Polycarbonate
Colour: Light Blue, Grey
Team: Francesco Dompieri
Time: 2011
Client: Foscarini

118. Metalco, Baia, 2020

Like an inlet at the edge of the city street, Baia ('bay') is a modular system of platforms that redefines the concept of parklet. Moving away from the temporary aesthetic of urban furniture by focusing on the habits and needs of those who live in the city, it offers a series of functional elements to create areas with a warm, welcoming feeling, where nature is integrated and inspires the design. →

119. Nichetto Studio, A Cookie for All, 2020

In response to the Covid-19-related global lockdowns, Nichetto Studio designed a downloadable cookie-making kit to offer everyone a moment of happiness. Inspired by Italian wooden chopping boards, the shape of the cookie symbolizes the act of sharing, as well as allowing easy dunking in jam, hazelnut spread and other favourite dips. The accompanying roller is patterned on Merletto lace from Burano, fully taking advantage of the opportunities provided by 3D printing technology. →

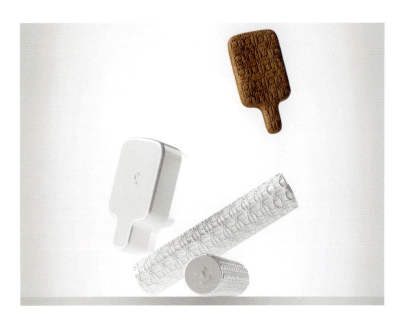

120. Rolf Benz, Liv, 2020

This sofa system is designed to address the many needs of a contemporary living room, with endless possibilities that allow the user always to obtain the right combination. Embodying an encounter between German quality and technological accuracy and the warmth of welcoming comfort that characterizes the Italian tradition of upholstery, Liv finds in geometric rigour the formula of its modularity. →

121. Rubelli, Carnevale Collection, 2020

With the mysterious charm of its masks and costumes and its festive atmosphere, the Venice Carnival has for centuries offered a show that is known all over the world. The Carnevale collection takes its cue from elements of this unique tradition and transfers them to the surfaces of three textiles: Coriandoli S, Coriandoli XL and Festa. All facilitated by Rubelli's craftsmanship in weaving. →

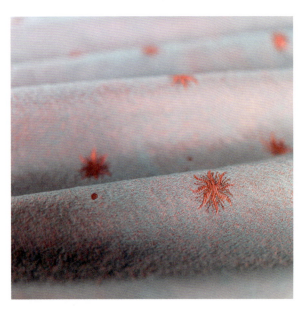

122. W-Eye, Avenue, 2020

With an impeccable fit and surprising lightness, the design of these spectacle frames is characterized by a sober and minimal elegance, with the roundness of the front frame meeting the temples seamlessly. The juxtaposition and combination of layers of wood and aluminium guarantee stability of the structure and offer a refined detail. Driven by the desire for personalized eyewear for everyday use, Avenue is available in the classic neutral and dark tones or with a contrasting inner frame in red. →

123. Wendelbo, Aloe, 2020–21

Like the plant from which it takes its name, the Aloe lounge chair makes contrast the distinctive feature of its elegant design. A tubular metal frame supports the chair and the upholstery seems to float as a natural continuation of the structure. Smooth and tensioned, the outer surface of the shell contrasts with an inner section of great softness. A stitching detail runs along all edges, its curve suggesting lightness as if effortlessly bent. →

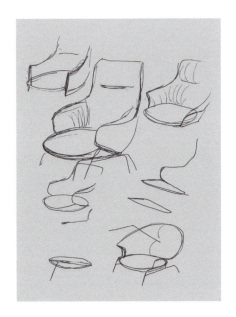

124. Wendelbo, Cinder Block, 2020

Designed as a set of blocks to be combined, Cinder Block is a modular sofa system that allows an almost infinite variety of settings through a small number of elements. The geometric rigour of the rectangular armrests and backrests contrasts with the softness of the cushions, which consist of two joined pieces: a pillow sewn to a high-density cylindrical element, guaranteeing the proper back support. A tray composed of an inner metal plate covered in leather offers a support surface that is easily applicable to both armrests and backrests. →

THINK OF A REGION LIKE A HUGE FACTORY

LORIS TESSARO IN CONVERSATION WITH FRANCESCA PICCHI

Think of a Region Like a Huge Factory.
Loris Tessaro in conversation with
Francesca Picchi

Francesca Picchi: I confess to a certain difficulty in defining your role. You're a product manager, meaning you're in charge of product industrialization, but in reality your work is pretty well unique in its field. I would describe you as a privileged observer of production in this region with such strong industrial capacity: a whole region organized as one huge factory. You were born in the Veneto, like Luca. You worked together from the start, wand the beginnings of Luca's career coincide with yours in research and development. How would you describe the working method you've developed together?

Loris Tessaro: I started working with Luca in the years when I'd just been made head of research and development at Casamania, an experimental company with some capital to invest and great ambition to grow. That was when we met, around 2004. Our relationship developed as we worked together and it has lasted through the years, despite changes in the company ownership and the places where we live and work. Luca went to Sweden and I moved to another company. In short, it's a relationship that grew out of making, sharing research into the best possible manufacturing methods, finding suppliers, materials and techniques suited to a specific concept, racking our brains to devise solutions, swapping ideas and even arguing … It's that type of closeness that develops through working together, and it gradually grew into friendship.

We're now working on a new project for a new brand, La Manufacture, part of the Cider Group. It's a project that links French, or rather Parisian, culture with manufacturing done wholly in Italy. It's a demanding project because it involves a complete catalogue of new products and the ambition to fuse design with fashion. Each product has a sort of ID card enabling you to trace its origin and who made it.

This project grew out of our urge to start from scratch and put all our commitment and heart into it, and I'm astonished at everything we've achieved in these two and a half years, with all the problems caused by social distancing. We curated twenty products in the first year and now we're about to come out with twenty-four new ones.

You can do this only if you're really on the same wavelength.

Luca is fortunate to have an international outlook, and he's taken his way of doing things to a global level by working with typically Italian companies in a very close relationship with work and production, a model he's managed to replicate in other contexts.

FP: As an expert in industrialization, you have a crucial role in design that I don't think can be learned at school.

LT: In Veneto there's a whole understorey of industrial companies, made up of subcontractors, suppliers and outsourcers who cover the full 360 degrees, from very advanced technology, such as carbon processing, to aluminium extrusion, die-casting, plastic injection-moulding … At the same time, alongside firms that aim continuously at technological innovation, some very gifted craftspeople still survive. It's not hard to find a carpenter who works in solid wood, an upholsterer with sartorial skills, a leatherworker … I don't know all the sectors, but I'd say it's a very complex field with an outstanding level of craftsmanship.

FP: How would you desribe this outstanding level craftsmanship?

LT: I mean there are companies that, despite being engaged in manufacturing, still preserve a part of that craft knowledge and passion in-house and apply it to help you find solutions, even when large production runs aren't involved. It's a mentality that leads them to behave the way a tailor does, making things to measure.

Ultimately, by craftsmanship I mean people willing to experiment, especially in the design phase. Not companies that don't want to think outside the box, and say, 'It can't be done.'

FP: If you had to choose one of Luca's projects that typifies the partnership you've developed, which would it be?

LT: The Jerry lamp, the first project we worked on together. I'm not sure it's my favourite, but it was the start of everything. When Luca showed up at Casamania we were both little more than youngsters. We were not so much product manager and designer, respectively, as a pair of dreamers, and together we managed to do something innovative by putting a lot of determination into it. There was that kind of excitement that young people have in making a new product, and this ended up becoming a tie between us, the start of a friendship. Even though we've made a lot of other products together, that first one has stayed in my heart. It was a fairly complex project and pretty innovative at the time because we were working with the cutting-edge technology of injection-moulded silicone. The lamp made in one piece resembled a lantern in shape, with a big hook that meant it could be hung anywhere, indoors or out, and it had to comply with a host of lighting regulations. The most exciting part was the technological challenge and developing the mould, which involved a whole series of complications. It was a challenge. And then there was the raw material. There was a single factory capable of producing it in Brescia, which specialized in making cake moulds.

It was a very interesting first approach, both for me as the head of research and development, and for the company, which Luca and I kept urging to have the courage to make a substantial investment in the moulds. And it was far from predictable that they would, given that Luca was very young at the time and not an established designer. But he talked everyone into it, because he's also an excellent salesman and very knowledgeable about all the factors involved, and understands the market.

The next step was an even more ambitious project: an injection-moulded plastic chair. That meant another substantial investment. Not all companies are ready to make an investment running to hundreds of thousands of euros in moulds, whether for injection-moulding or die-casting, for a project by a young designer.

It was a great experience. We called it Stereo [2008] because we were among the first to use the stereolithography technique to make the model, before starting production of the mould. It was a family of chairs, made from an injection-moulded shell in various versions, from one with four wooden legs to another with tubular legs and yet another with a sledge base, with or without armrests, to an office seat and a swivel chair. It was an industrial product that involved a lot of different suppliers. For this reason we studied all the details to simplify assembly as well as shipping, since it was designed for the contract sector. We had set ourselves the goal of perfect industrial production. To eliminate screws and facilitate assembly, we decided to join the parts simply by pressure. We devised a special bayonet joint to attach the legs to the seat. Firmly bonding metal to plastic wasn't easy, and we invented some rather complex mould slides. Since we wanted to keep the price affordable, we worked to make the shell as thin as possible so that moulding times would be fast and the cost competitive. In this respect, the design of the two flanges that bend slightly also served as ribbing to stiffen the body and enable us to work with a thickness of just 8 mm. As I said, it was a very substantial investment and it has borne fruit, but if you think of the potential it had, perhaps the company was never ready to exploit it fully.

FP: Luca maintains that industrialization is a school. What do you think?

LT: The process of industrialization is also a human experience that leads you to learn a little about everything, but above all it teaches you to really engage with the people working in the different sectors throughout the various stages of the process. This is because upholstery, like woodworking or printing, has its own language. Each has its own mindset, its own secrets. That kind of close teamwork created by people making things together brings enormous advantages to production, because ultimately products must have a soul, and the soul is the result of all the individual contributions made by everyone who works on the project.

Loris Tessaro has long been involved in research and development. A Venetian, he has worked for Casamania and other companies in the Veneto region. The manufacturing experience he has built up make him one of the leading experts in the industrial fabric of the Italian North East. Over the years he has put together a network of skilled Italian artisans with whom he has established a solid and lasting relationship. He has also collaborated with many designers on the international scene including Patrick Norguet, Karim Rashid, Claesson Koivisto Rune, nendo, Konstantin Grcic and Ronan and Erwan Bouroullec. Today he works for the French brand La Manufacture, of which Luca Nichetto is art director.

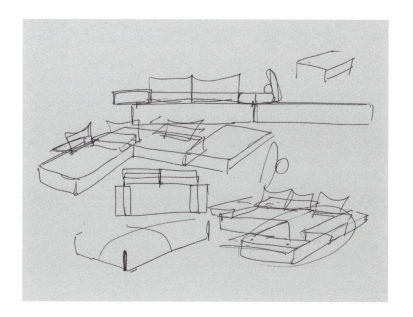

125. Wendelbo, Sepal, 2020

Characterized by the harmonious balance between aesthetic and functionality, Sepal is a family composed of a sofa, a lounge chair, dining chairs and a dining table. The enveloping soft shapes of the upholstery enhance the comfort of the seat while the metal structure, by avoiding sharp angles, suggests a welcoming feeling of elegance and constitutes a distinctive design detail that marks the entire family. →

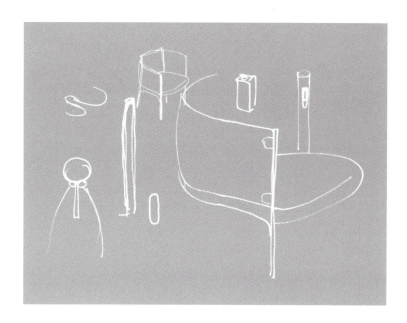

126. Conterie, Mecha, 2021

Three small modern, colourful glass robots evoking Japanese icons in rustproof and glittering armour are an essence of antitheses, the wonder of creativity. They were designed for *Empathic: Discovering a Glass Legacy* (2021–2022), an exhibition at Murano's InGalleria/Punta Conterie Art Gallery curated by Luca Nichetto, whose aim was to celebrate and promote the expertise and experimentation of the island's most famous craft. →

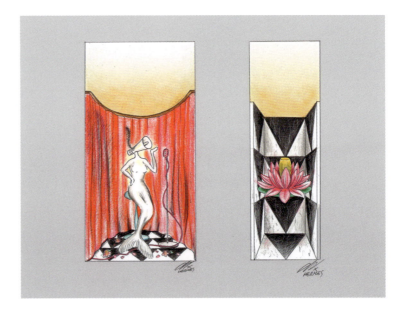

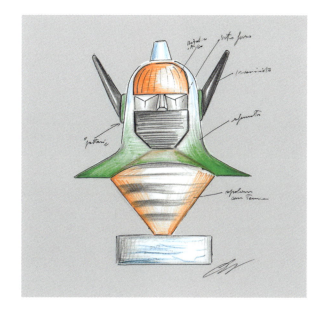

127. Hermès, Mythological Renaissance, Milan, 2021

Hermès commissioned Luca Nichetto to create the first *vitrines d'artistes* for the maison's renovated store in via Montenapoleone, Milan, interpreting the Hermès theme for 2021 – 'A Human Odyssey' – through an art journey of four mythological tales revisited in a surreal tone. This is a journey that takes visitors through architectural references and imaginary charms, following the neon thread that connects the four sets, made with materials that merge Parisian creativity with Italian *savoir faire*. →

128. La Manufacture, Allié, 2021

A dual-purpose object, Allié is both a stool and a side table that exudes character within a small package. The integral skin polyurethane-moulded top and rigid polyurethane foam base are connected by two metal handles that give it a strong structure and allow it to be moved around easily. The matte finish of the main body contrasts with the metal finish of the handles, which, along with the contemporary colour palette, complete the vision of this playful and fun object. →

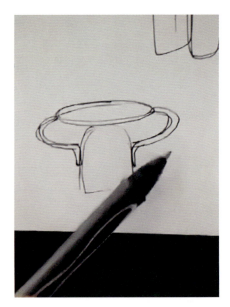

129. La Manufacture, Fashion Collection, 2021

More than twenty womenswear and menswear pieces showcase oversized cuts, conjuring up 90s-style streetwear vibes, while prints, textures and colour palettes draw inspiration from La Manufacture's furniture collections. The pieces bear clearly identifiable patches, reminiscent of those worn by sports or music fans. →

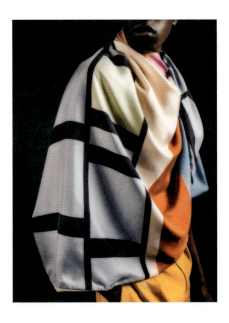

PROJECT 020
OFFECCT
ROBO

Project 020: Offecct, Robo

Sustainability has become a hot topic across many industries, but I had never felt it so relevant and present in my job until I landed a partnership with the Swedish furniture design company Offecct.

On 8 February 2007 I was in the city to celebrate my then fiancée's birthday, and toured the Stockholm Furniture Fair, where I discovered several companies that were shaping the Scandinavian design ethos. In particular, Offecct piqued my curiosity and I started doing my research to get in touch with Anders Englund, the company's co-founder and design manager.

In the year after meeting Anders I came across an Italian manufacturer of motorcycle saddles, crafted using the rotational moulding technique. This fortuitous encounter ignited my creativity and prompted me to propose to Offecct a padded bench, in light of the company's long-standing involvement in public-space projects.

Despite the communication gap caused by my lack of fluency in English back then, Anders wanted to pursue the project. He even flew to Italy to meet the supplier and see at first hand the polystyrene life-size model. After two weeks of radio silence, Anders came back to me regretful that the project did not match Offecct's standards in terms of carbon footprint and environmental responsibility. The company's ethos was and is rooted in creating true value for people and society. Each product had to have that magical, elusive spark that can make the world a better place.

Based on those premises, my focus shifted entirely to references as diverse as the human body and robot characters seen in Japanese manga and anime. The latter became quite a fixation after I watched Chris Cunningham's music video for Björk's 'All Is Full of Love' (1999), in which a couple of robots gain human and emotional qualities, ultimately kissing and hugging.

I envisioned a chair with visible junctions, based on a Thonet design, and whose components could be easily disassembled and stowed in a compact box for transportation. Again, I had probably not grasped the breadth of the company's sustainable policies and initially proposed materials – a composite made of wood and plastic – that did not match Offecct's expectations.

After a year of research I found a bentwood manufacturer on the outskirts of Udine, Italy, who brought the first prototype for the Robo chair to life in just three months. Pairing this with Finnish felt crafted from recycled PET bottles, I presented the chair to the Offecct team, pulling each component out of the box and assembling it before their eyes.

The chair stole the spotlight at the Stockholm Furniture Fair in 2010, although it never gained much commercial traction. But the collaboration helped put me on the Swedish and international design radar, all the while pushing me to embed a product's life-cycle assessment in my design practice.

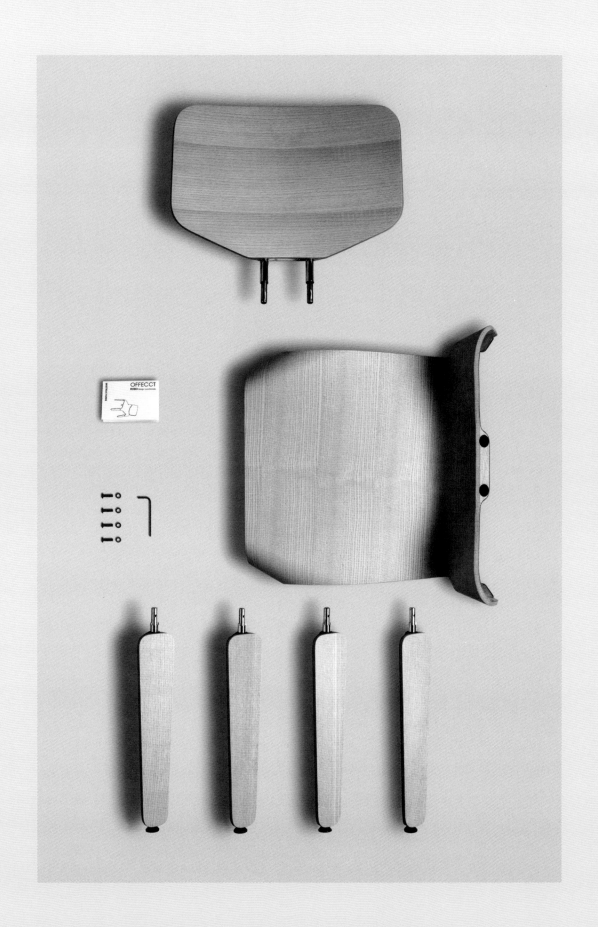

Type: Stackable Chair
Material: Ash wood, PET felt, Metal
Colour: Black, White
Team: Francesco Dompieri, Matteo Fogale, Paolo Da Ponte
Time: 2010
Client: Offecct

130. La Manufacture, Val, 2021

Designed as a contemporary outdoor armchair of the kind that is seen in many outdoor environments, and rotomoulded in plastic, Val contrasts its scooped-out seating with angular side walls that allow it to be arranged in organic clusters. The central hole is functional, allowing water to drain away during inclement weather. →

131. Artifort Glider, 2021

With its organic design, Glider offers an attractive, relaxed seating experience in lobbies and lounges. The generous seat with shapely arm wings, the blind joint connecting the frame to the seat shells, the elegant stitching and the rich choice of fabrics and leather lend allure and authenticity to the design. →

132. Stellar Works, Space Invaders Collection, 2021

Celebrating the first collaboration between Nichetto Studio and Stellar Works, Space Invaders is an eclectic collection of objects with different functions and a bold character. Table lamps, rechargeable lamps, small tables with integrated lights, and trays find their own aesthetic in the juxtaposition of materials and shapes that interpenetrate each other, marking an 'invasion of space' that creates an original modularity. →

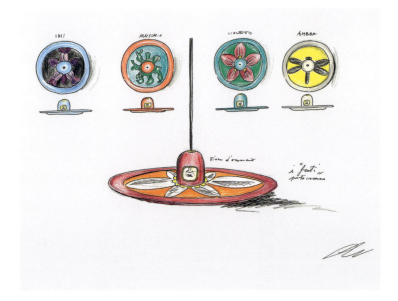

134. Bernhardt Design, Nico, 2021

The chair is a throwback to the mid-century space-age design aesthetic; it has an exceptionally distinctive composition and stance. Formed from two inverted conical shapes, the bottom rises to create a wide centre point, while the backrest continues to narrow as it reaches the top of the chair. The exterior is rigid, while the interior is covered with soft moulded foam to achieve maximum comfort. Generous flanges separate the upper and lower sections where they meet and continue to trace the arms and back silhouette. →

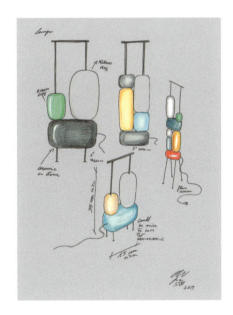

133. Ginori 1735, LCDC Collection, 2021

Ginori 1735's first foray into home fragrances, the LCDC Collection – La Compagnia di Caterina – draws inspiration from Lucha Libre (Mexican wrestling) masks, the illustrations of Jean-Paul Goude and graffiti art. In Luca Nichetto's creative vision, the statuesque faces of the characters become the archetypal protagonists of the collection. Thanks to the design, which blends the classicism of ancestral statues with rigorous lines, the faces and sculptures take on a mysterious, iconic dimension. (See page 47.)

135. Angela Roi, Malala, 2022

Designed around an idea of interpreting the concept of the 'cabinet of curiosities' as a carry-all bag, filled with a personal and richly varied array of items. A pocket-lined perimeter defines the shape of the bag, and offers endless possibilities for compartmentalized organization. Dimensions are dictated by the items most commonly found in a woman's bag, and the aesthetics are rooted in aligning with the style of a modern, independent professional woman. Malala comes in three different sizes to easily accompany both day and evening events. →

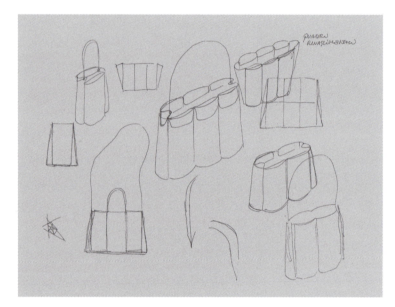

LOOKING OUTSIDE THE SMALL GARDEN OF ITALIAN DESIGN

FRANCESCO DOMPIERI IN CONVERSATION WITH MAX FRASER

Looking Outside the Small Garden of Italian Design.
Francesco Dompieri in conversation with
Max Fraser

Max Fraser: You've been working with Luca since 2007. How did that come about?

Francesco Dompieri: I was at university for my second degree, and one day one of my teachers, Alessandro Pedron, met me in a corridor and simply told me, 'there's a friend of mine in Venice who is looking for someone in his studio to replace a person who is leaving.' I called Luca with the expectation of maybe a summer job or an internship. He had a look at my portfolio, then invited me to the studio, and he told me he needed someone who wanted to grow with the studio, which was developing a lot at that stage. It was at the very beginning of Luca becoming kind of famous in the industry.

MF: What was your experience of walking into that studio straight from university?

FD: It was an exciting moment; when you're at university, you don't know anything about real life. I started in 2007 learning everything I didn't learn during my student years. I really didn't know anything about anything, including all the parts of the work that are not usually written about in the magazines: contracts, royalties, how to be paid by clients, how to get jobs from clients, and stuff like that.

During the first period working with Luca, I was a bit scared because his way is different from the normal Italian way. Normally, they try to teach you and then see if you can put what you've learned into practice. With Luca, it was a bit different; he encouraged me to do the things that I'm able to do as well as the things that I'm not able to do, because he is of the belief that we learn by making errors. It was a very important learning period for Luca too.

MF: What is your working relationship within the studio?

FD: We became business partners in 2011 after the opening of the studio in Stockholm. I manage the office in Venice. It's hard to find a definition for what I do because I often jump from one task to another. Luca and I always talk before taking on a new client, but time is our worst enemy and there are occasions when we don't talk for several days. I oversee most of the projects that we are doing as a studio. I've got a practical role; I'm more specialized in developing the project following the first presentation to the client. I work on the second phase, when the client is developing prototypes and making revisions, as well as when suppliers need advice. That is also my favourite part. In this phase, Luca taught me a lot about the way to behave with suppliers and clients.

MF: You've been business partners for so long, but the name above the door is Nichetto and Luca is the public face. You are the crucial right-hand man to Luca, so I'm interested in your working dynamic.

FD: Of course, he is the founder of the studio and more than eighty per cent of the ideas that come out of the studio are from his sketches. Most of all, he has a strong ability to speak with people and to develop a network. Without this network, it would be impossible for the studio to be at the level that we are now.

I'm more of a desk guy; a lot of the time I translate Luca's sketches on to the computer and communicate with new suppliers. After fifteen years, I can understand what is in his mind, so I can be faster than others to put his ideas into practice, occasionally adding my touch.

MF: You used to work opposite each other in the Venice studio. Since he moved to Stockholm, how has the distance changed things?

FD: For the first two or three years, Luca was moving back and forth between studios every two weeks. We had time to get used to being far away. But I miss the relationship with Luca. There's not much time to speak and to have a relationship after work. In the past we used to make time for a drink in a bar. Like any kind of significant friendship, he was the person with whom I spent the most time.

MF: What do you consider to be some of the most important chapters in the evolution of the studio?

FD: Talking about products, the most important that I remember is when we worked with Cassina. For a young designer, receiving a call from Cassina is like God calling you on the phone! Even if the product is now out of production, we learned so much from this great company. They have an office that is dedicated entirely to research and development, with people who understand the design culture. At that time Ferdinando Mussi (see pages 191–193) was in charge of that office. He and his team gave our product the importance that sometimes smaller or newer companies can't give. During those six months, I learned most [of what] I know about upholstery.

Another project I remember is the Robo chair (see pages 217–222). We developed it inside the studio because the client, Offecct, gave us total freedom. We did it entirely in Italy, which allowed Luca and me to visit the facility of a plywood supplier, where we experienced the moulding process. This was an important step for me from a technical point of view.

An experience that gave me a lot of pleasure was the Prosciutteria exhibition in Milan in 2011 (see page 44). The prosciutto brand King's commissioned us to design the whole space as well as new cutting knives, all of the clothing for the staff, and the branding together with a graphic designer. It was a comprehensive experience and an important step for me.

And there's an evolving chapter, which is our relationship with Loris Tessaro. I first met him in 2007 when he was working at Casamania, and we continue to work with him today through La Manufacture. He has been another great teacher over the years, always ready to share information, tricks of the trade, contacts with great suppliers and much more.

More broadly, the other key chapter was when we became known in the rest of the world. At the very beginning we were working only with Italian clients, then in 2011 Luca started working with Nordic companies, and then brands from other countries came along.

Being able to look outside the small garden of Italian design is an opportunity that a lot of other designers of the same age don't have. This is probably the most important factor that made our studio what it is right now. Initially, it was extremely hard to be part of the Italian design community because we weren't in Milan. Milan bills itself as the only capital of design in the world, and it is like an exclusive club of designers – you can't get in. Luca was smart to understand that there was the rest of the world to be designed.

MF: What would you say are Luca's strengths and weaknesses?

FD: He has a strong vision – even after so long, I'm still not able to anticipate what he will draw on a piece of paper! Another strength is that he can speak to anyone and make himself understood. When he first went to Sweden, he couldn't even speak English, but he found a way to be understood and to convince people that we were the studio to work with. Language aside, he was an early adopter of online communication and one of the first to place importance on social media as a way to spread [awareness of] the work of the studio. Also, Luca is very precise with details. He wants to have a look at every single screw in a project. He is totally dedicated to the work.

Sometimes he doesn't have patience and sometimes he either loves or hates something or someone, but I can't say that he has many weaknesses.

MF: If you had to describe the work of the studio to somebody you'd never met before, how would you explain not just the diversity of work that you do, but also the Nichetto DNA?

FD: I'd say that each project we've done from the beginning until now has always had the human touch. We never do things that are cold or only functional. We always try to add a human sensibility. We design products that we like and that we want to have around us.

MF: Knowing the ecological impact of putting more products into the world, how does a designer remain relevant today?

FD: There's a lot of contradictions around these issues. You have to invest part of your time in researching new uses of materials as well as the future needs of people. However, spending time doing this research probably won't give you the money to pay the rent, so then you're forced to design more products that will sell well. There's a contradiction because you have to do both.

Perhaps the way to remain relevant is to strive to design good and long-lasting products that are also good sellers. This has always been the goal, but now the attention has shifted to new materials with convincing green credentials, and also the hunt for new ways to interact with objects or with non-physical products.

MF: What has kept you working with Luca for all these years?

FD: I have developed a strong link to the studio and I'm dedicated to the path we are pursuing. There was a moment when I could've decided to become an independent designer or continued to be part of something greater; I chose to be part of something greater. If someone asks me, 'but why are you still there?' … well, I married the project!

Francesco Dompieri and Luca Nichetto have been working together since 2007, initially while Francesco was still completing his training as an industrial designer at Università Iuav di Venezia. Today he is a business partner of Nichetto Studio, stationed at the studio in Venice, where he manages many of the technical elements of the studio's projects, as well as production and client liaison. Luca Nichetto describes Francesco Dompieri as a sort of brother to him as he has been an integral part of the studio's growth.

136. Barovier & Toso, Vallonné, 2022

Vallonné highlights the production capabilities of mouth-blown glass, integrating organic and unexpected patterns in a cohesive union. Sinuous shapes are further highlighted by two material finish options, transparent and opaque. →

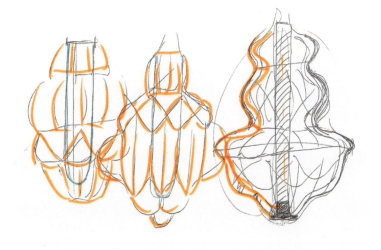

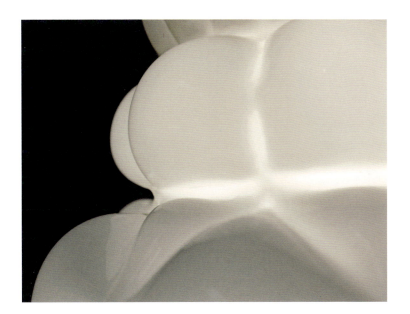

137. Steinway & Sons, Gran Nichetto, 2022

Celebrating beauty, craftsmanship and history, Gran Nichetto is at first a sculpture that celebrates the know-how and iconic nature of the Steinway & Sons brand. Designed to emphasize the brand's substance and soul with a contemporary twist, Gran Nichetto cuts corners and surfaces, synchronizes matte and polished surfaces and interplays light and reflection as though everything harmonizes and dances with the music. (See page 27.)

INDEX

Index

Page numbers in *italics* refer to illustrations.

A. W. Bauer & Co. 48
    Ombra Delle 5 80, *80*
Aarnio, Eero 131
ADI (Association of Industrial Design) 124
Affetto Collection 43, *43*
Afra 128
Algon 102, *102*
Allié 215, *215*, *216*
Aloe 208, *208*
Alphabeta 100, *100–101*
&Tradition: Cloud 100, *101*, *101*
    Isole 117, *117*, *118*
    Lato 136, *136*
Angela Roi, Malala 226, *226*
Arflex 22
    Algon 102, *102*
    Capilano 102, *102*, *109*
    Ladle 64, *71*
    Papoose 82, *82*, 101
    Serena and Doge 71, *71*
    Supplì 195, *195*
    Tellin 141, *141*
Arillo 36, *36*, *37*
Armento, Gianluca 182
Artifort: Glider 224, *224*, *225*
    Pala *118*, 119, *119*
Astro 161, *161*, *162*
Aureola 72, 73, *73*
Avenue 206, *206*, *207*

B&B Italia 20, 128, 146, 192, 194
B/Side Design 140
Badii, Alessandro 48, 57–60
Baia 205, *205*
Barovier & Toso, Vallonné 231, *231*
Bcool 35, *35*
Beatrice, Hanna Nova 164
Beijing Design Week 96, 138–139, 140
Belle Reeve 170, *171*, *171*
Bernhardt Design: Luca Collection 170, *170*, *171*
    Nico 224, *225*
Bianco, Renato 48, *59*
Björk 37, 218
Blanche 80, *80*, *81*, 111
Blasco, Gandía, Onde 198, *198*
Bosa Ceramiche: Essence Collection 24, *25*, *25*
    Hook Box 16, *17*, *17*
    Umbravase 16, *16–17*
Botswana 73
Bouroullec, Ronan and Erwan 123, 212

Branzi, Andrea 9–10
BTM (Breaking the Mould) 84, 115, 116
Bubble 14, *14*, *15*
Burano 205
Busnelli, Piero 192, 193
Byredo 48, 104

Calder, Alexander 144
Canal 135, *135*, *136*
Capilano 102, *102*, *109*
Cappellin, Luigi 146
Cappellini 22, 123
Carnevale Collection 206, *206*, *207*
Casamania 210, 212, 229
    Jerry 10
    Nuance 24, *25*, *25*
    Stereo 23, *23*
Cassina 122, 192–3, 194, 228
    La Mise 54, *54–55*, *181–186*
    Motek 55, *55*, 193
    Torei 46, *46*, 193
Cassina, Cesare 192, 194
Castaño-López, Esther and Elena 66
Castiglioni, Achille 9, 122
Castle, Wendell 40
Cavandoli, Osvaldo 62
Censer 134, *135*, *135*
China Art Archives and Warehouse 140
Choy, Yoko 95–98
Cinder Block 208, *208*, *209*
Citterio, Antonio 122
Claesson, Mårten 22
Claesson Koivisto Rune 22, 212
Classy Collection 196, *196*, *197*
Cloud 100, *100*, *101*
Coedition: MDW Stand *118*, 119, *119*
    Paris Showroom 141, *141*, *142*, *143*
    You Sofa 120, *120*
Collective Contemporist 98
Colombo, Carlo 123
Constellations 144, *144*
Conterie, Mecha 214, *214*, *215*
A Cookie for All 205, *205*, *206*
Coppola, Sofia 48
Cunningham, Chris 37, 218

Danish Color Board 78
Dart 18, *18*
Das Haus 56, *56*, *61*
De La Espada 48
    Belle Reeve 170, *171*, *171*
    Blanche 80, *80*, *81*, 111
    Dubois 80, *81*, 82
    Elysia 70, 79, 110, 111
    Harold 91, *91*
    Kim 109, *109*
    Laurel 91, *91*, *92*
    Marlon 92, *93*, *93*

  Mitch 92, 93, *93*
  Nino 110, *110*, *111*
  Stanley 94, *94*, *109*
  Steve 109, *109*, *110*
  Vivien 94, *94*, *95*
De Padova 122
Decode/Recode 104
Design House 44, *44*, *45*, 229
Dixon, Tom 104
DND, Viva 195, *195*, *196*
Dompieri, Francesco 150, 186, 222, 227–230
Dordoni, Rodolfo 122
The Dream Carousel 172, *172*
Dubois 80, *80*, *81*, *82*

Easy Peasy 190, *190*
Elysia 79, *79*, *110*, *111*
Empathic: Discovering a Glass Legacy (2021–2022) 214
Englund, Anders 122, 218
Ericson, Estrid 160
Esedra Sunbed 110, *111*, *111*, *112*
Essence Collection 24, *25*, *25*
Established & Sons, Golconda 46, *46*, *47*
Et al, Classy Collection 196, *196*, *197*
Ethimo: Esedra Sunbed 110, *111*, *111*, *112*
  Pluvia 133, *133*
  Venexia 196, *197*, *197*

Face 16, *16*, *17*
Fashion Collection 216, *216*, 223
Float 55, *55*, *56*
Floema 169, *169*
Fogia: Jord 133, *133*, *134*
  Luft 134, *135*, *135*
  Mame 142, *143*, *143*
  Print Test 142, *143*, *143*
Fontana Arte 22
Fornasarig, Wolfgang Collection 38, *38*
Foscarini 10, 122, 124
  Kurage 99, *99*, *100*
  O-Space 14, *15*, *15*
  Plass 10, 45, *45*, 199–204
  Stewie 53, *53*, *54*
  Troag 26, *26*
Frank, Josef 160
Fusa 160, *160*, *161*

Gai, Gianpietro 14, 15, 122, 200
Gallery Pascale, Les Poupées 54, *54*, *55*
Gardone, Massimo 80
Gemo 154, *154*, *159*
Geoart 26, *26*
Ginori 1735, LCDC Collection 47–52, 58–59, 60, 226, *226*, 224, *225*
Glider 224, *224*, *225*
The Global School 140
Globo, Affetto Collection 43, *43*

Golconda 46, *46*, *53*
Gorham, Ben 48, 104, 108
Goude, Jean-Paul 48, 225
Gran Nichetto 27–34, 40–41, 231, *231*
Grcic, Konstantin 212
Greenpads 43, *43*, *44*

Hai 72, *72*, *73*
Halo 112, *112*
Harold 91, *91*
Hem: Alphabeta 100, *100*, *101*
  Hai 72, *72*, *73*
Heritage 160, *160*, *161*
Hermès: The Dream Carousel 115, 172, *172*
  Mythological Renaissance 214, 215
  Pure Imagination, Venice 83–90, 115, 143, *143*
Hirst, Damien 28
Hook Box 16, 17, *17*
Hutten, Richard 156

Iacchetti, Giulio 10
Icesac 24, *24*, *25*
IMM Cologne, Das Haus 56, *56*, *61*
InGalleria/Punta Conterie Art Gallery 214
Intercolor 78
Interiors on Stage 56
Isole 117, *117*, *118*, *119*
Università Iuav di Venezia (IUAV) 7, 9, 104, 130, 200, 230
Italesse: Bcool 35, *35*
  Icesac 24, *24*, *25*
  Stripe 18, *18*
  Titan 23, *23*
  Venti4 Set 35, *35*, *36*

Jerry 10, 210
Jord 133, *133*, *134*
Juhl, Finn 78

Kapoor, Anish 104
Kartell 123
Kering Group 60
Kim 109, *109*
Knight, Anthony 66
Knives 44, 45, *45*
Koivisto, Eero 19–21, 22
Kravitz, Lenny 28
Kristalia 122
  Constellations 144, *144*
  Dart 18, *18*
  Face 16, *16*, *17*
  Plate 46/50 24, *24*, *25*
  Tenso 151, *151*
Kurage 99, *99*, *100*
Kuramata, Shirō 164

La Chance, Float 54, 55, *55*
La Manufacture 210, 212, 229

Allié 215, *215*, 216
  Fashion Collection 216, *216*, 223
  Luizet 177, *177*
  Melitea 177, *177*, *178*
  Olindias *178*, 179, *179*
  Pyrite *178*, 179, *179*
  Showroom 3 Rue Edouard VII 179, *179*, *180*
  Soufflé 180, *180*
  Tima 187, *187*
  Val 223, *223*
La Mise 54, *54–55*, 181–186
Laboratorio 2729 25
Ladle 64, *64*, 71
Lagerfeld, Karl 28, 40
Land Rover, Censer *134*, 135, *135*
Lato 136, *136*
Laurel 91, *91*, 92
LCDC Collection 47–52, 58–59, 60, 224, 225
Leanza, Beatrice 96, 137–140
Legato 152, *152*, *153*
Les Poupées 54, *54*, 55
Lilin 169, *169*
Linea 62, *62*, 63
Lissoni, Piero 122
Liv 206, *206*, 207
Living Divani 20, 122–123
Loch Ness 187
Lodes, Easy Peasy 190, *190*
London Design Festival 174
London Plastics Fair 192
Lovegrove, Ross 104
Luca Collection 170, *170*, 171
Luft *134*, 135, *135*
Luhrmann, Baz 48
Luizet 177, *177*

Mabeo, Pula 72, *73*, 73
Magis 123
Magistretti, Vico 122, 182
Magritte, René 46
Maison&Objet 48, 174
Malala 226, *226*
Mame *142*, 143, *143*
Mari, Enzo 127
Marlon 92, *93*, 93
Matter Made: Legato 152, *152*, *153*
  Rotea 152, *152*, *153*
Maurer, Ingo 104
MDW Stand 118, *119*, *119*
Mecha 214, *214*, *215*
Medici, Catherine de' 48, 58–59
Melitea 177, *177*, *178*
Memphis group 9
Metalco, Baia 205, *205*
Milan 7, 9, 10, 20, 66, 120, 122, 215, 229

Milan Design Week 44, 48, 63, 104, 115, 125
Millebolle 9, 14, *14*, *15*, 104, 114
Minotti 20, 122–123
Miró, Joan 144
Mitch 92, *93*, 93
Mjölk Collection, Aureola 72, *73*, 73
Mjölk Collection, Sucabaruca 73, *73*–74
Mjölk Collection, Uki 74, *74*
Moiseeva, Lera 72, 73
Molteni 122
Monitillo Marmi, Nessie 187, *187*, *188*
Moooi: Canal 135, *135*, *136*
  Reflections 152, *153*
Moore, Simon 104, 114
Moroso 122
Motek 55, *55*, 56, 193
Murano 7, 9, 36, 45, 74, 84, 97, 104, 113–116, 122, 136, 138, 152, 160, 172, 200, 214
Murano (Offecct chair) 154, *154*
Mussi, Ferdinando 182, 191–194, 229
Mythological Renaissance 214, *215*

NasonMoretti 84
  Halo 112, *112*
nendo 99, 117, 156, 174–5, 212
  Nichetto = nendo 62, 63, 163–8
Nessie 187, *187*, *188*
New York Design Week 28, 40
Next Stop 65–70, 76–77, 162, *162*
Nichetto, Åsa 7, 20, 122, 123
Nichetto = nendo 62, 63, 163–168
Nichetto Studio, A Cookie for All 205, *205*, 206
Nichetto Workshop 188, *188*, *189*
Nico 224, *224*, *225*, 226
Nino 110, *110*, *111*
Nodus by Il Piccolo: Geoart 26, *26*
  Regata Storica 61, *62*, 63
Norguet, Patrick 212
Notes 127
Novembre, Fabio 122, 123
Nuance 24, 25, *25*

O-Space 14, *15*, *15*, 200
Offecct 22, 122
  Greenpads 43, *43*, 44
  Linea 62, *62*, 63
  Murano 154, *154*
  Notes 127
  Phoenix 112, *112*, 117
  Robo 37, *37*, 122, 217–222, 229
Olindias *178*, 179, *179*
Ombra Delle 5 80, *80*, *81*
Onde 198, *198*
Orléans, Henri d' 48, 58–59
Otto 36, *36*, *37*

Paiano, Roberto 182
Pala 118, *119*, *119*

Palomba, Roberto 123, 156
Papoose 82, *82*
Parachilna, Gemo 154, *159*
Paris Design Week 135
Paris Showroom (Coedition) 141, *141*, *142*, *143*
Pavilion (Tales) 62, *62*, *63*, 64
Pedron, Alessandro 228
Pesce, Gaetano 193
Phoenix 112, *112*, *117*
Pijoulat, Claire 28
Plass 10, 44, *44*, 199–204
Plate 46/50 24, *24*, *25*
Pluvia 133, *133*
Polan, Robert 28, 39–42
Poliform 122–123
Ponti, Gio 48, 182
Prihnenko, Natacha 84
Print Test 142, 143, *143*
Prosciutteria King's: Design House 44, *44*, *45*, 229
    Knives 44, 45, *45*
Pula 72, *73*, 73
Punta Conterie 97, 214
Pure Imagination 83–90, 115, 143, *143*
Pyrae/Strata 84, 103–108, 120, *120*
Pyrite 178, *179*, *179*

Rashid, Karim 212
Ratatouille 159, *159*, *160*
Reflections 152, *153*
Regata Storica 61, *62*, *63*
Robo 37, *37*, 122, 217–222, 229
Rolf Benz, Liv 206, *206*, *207*
Roosegaarde, Daan 130
Rosholm, Marie-Louise 66, 75–78, 162
Rotea 152, *152*, *153*
Rubelli, Carnevale Collection 206, *206*, *207*
Rune, Ola 22

Sacchi, Luca 84
Sadler, Marc 200
Salone del Mobile, Milan 10, 76, 138
Salviati 84, 104, 115, 122, 124
    Bubble 14, *14*, *15*
    Millebolle 9, 14, *14*, *15*, 104, 114
    Pyrae/Strata 84, 103–108, 120, *120*
    Spoon 15, *15*
Sancal, Next Stop 65–70, 76–77, 162, *162*
Sarpaneva, Timo 54
Sato, Oki 63, 99, 164–168, 173–176
Scarpa, Afra and Tobia 128
Scarpa, Carlo 56
Sepal 213, *213*
Serena and Doge 71, *71*, *72*
Serenella Industria Vetraria 115
Showroom 3 Rue Edouard VII (La Manufacture) 179, *179*, *180*
Silk 146
Skultuna, Streamers 188, *189*, *189*

Sottsass, Ettore 9, 54, 122, 164
Soufflé 180, *180*
Space Invaders Collection 224, *224*, *225*
Stanley 94, *94*, 111
Starck, Philippe 123
Steinway & Sons, Gran Nichetto 27–34, 40–42, 231, *231*
Stellar Works, Space Invaders Collection 224, *224*, *225*
Stellon, Dario 84, 104, 113–116
Stereo 23, *23*, 211
Steve 110, *111*
Stewie 53, *53*, 54
Stockholm 10, 122, 123, 160, 228
Stockholm Furniture & Light Fair 122, 174, 218
    Ratatouille 159, *159*, *160*
Streamers 188, *189*, *189*
Stripe 18, *18*
Studio MLR 78
Studio Wolfgang 38
Sucabaruca 73, *73*, 74
Supplì 195, *195*
Svenskt Tenn: Fusa 160, *160*, *161*
    Heritage 160, *160*, *161*
Swedese 122

Tales, Pavilion 62, *62*, *63*, 64, 139
Tellin 141, *141*
Tenso 151, *151*
Tessaro, Loris 209–212, 229
Testa, Armando 73
Thonet, Michael 38, 218
Thorpe, Marc 28
Tiffany, Joseph Burr 40
Tima 187, *187*
Titan 23, *23*
Tokyo 2020 Olympics 164
Tokyo Design Week 174
Torei 46, *46*, 193
Triennale di Milano 9
Troag 26, *26*
Tubes, Astro 161, *161*, *162*

Uki 74, *74*
Umbravase 16, *16*–*17*
Urbinati, Carlo 200

Val 223, *223*
Vallonné 231, *231*
Vecchiato, Alessandro 'Sandro' 200
Vedel, Hanne 78
Venexia 196, *197*, *197*
Venice 7, 9, 36, 48, 61, 71, 84, 122, 135, 143, 228
Venice Architecture Biennale 96, 140
Venice Carnival 206
Venini 25
    Arillo 36, *36*, *37*
    Otto 36, *36*, *37*

Venini, Paolo 115
Venti4 Set 35, *35*, *36*
Vessel Gallery 25
Viva 195, *195*, *196*
Vivien 94, *94*, *99*

W-Eye, Avenue 206, *206*, *207*
Wallpaper* 98
WantedDesign 28
Wästberg 22
Wegner, Hans J. 38, 78
Wei, Shu 146, *155–158*
Wendelbo: Aloe 208, *208*
    Cinder Block 208, *208*, *213*
    Floema 169, *169*
    Lilin 169, *169*
    Sepal 213, *213*
Wittmann 96
    Nichetto Workshop 188, *188*, *189*
Wolfgang Collection 38, *38*

You 120, *120*

ZaoZuo 96, 97, *156–158*
    ZaoZuo Collection 79, *79*, *145–150*
Zucchi 48

Image credits

All sketches and prototype images are courtesy and copyright © Nichetto Studio.

Photographs are referred to by project number.

Francesco Allegretto for InGalleria/Punta Conterie Art Gallery: 126; Francis Amiand, Aurélien Chauvaud: 034; Archivio Venini: 022; Mattia Balsamini, Andrea Martinadonna, Maurizio Polese: 073; Barovier&Toso: 136; Luis Beltran, Jose Gandia-Blasco, Alejandra Gandia-Blasco, Odosdesign: 117; Rolf Benz: 120; Virgile Simon Bertrand: 101; Jonas Bjerre-Poulsen, Fogia: 075; Jonas Bjerre-Poulsen. Mathias Nero: 076; Irina Boersma, Anders Schønnemann: 060; Bosa Ceramiche: 005, 007, 013; BTM: 088; Casamania: 011, 014; S. Caleca, B. Brancato: 029; F. Cedrone, N. Zocchi: 035; Pietro Cocco, Studio Blanco: 129; Paolo Contratti: 006, 008, 012, 085, 086; François Coquerel: 106; De La Espada: 046, 049, 050, 052, 053, 054, 055, 056, 057, 063, 064, 065, 100; Massimo Gardone: 003, 009, 015, 017, 018, 019, 027, 028, 048, 115; Kasia Gatkowska: 058; Ivan Gonzalez: 134; Walter Gumiero, Arflex: 041, 042, 051, 061, 062; Thomas Harrysson: 090; Thomas Harrysson, Offecct: 068; Brooke Holm: 087; IKB, Thomas Pagani, Arflex: 113; Hiroshi Iwasaki: 038; Gustav Kaiser, Neni Studio: 092; Eric Laignel, Ivan Gonzalez: 099; Jesse Laitinen, Saša Antić: 135; Thomas Larcher: 010; Matthieu Lavanchy with set design by Cameranesi Pompili and art direction by Studio Blanco: 133; Erik Lefvander: 043, 059; Jonathan Leijonhufvud: 040; Andy Liffner, Studio Skultuna: 110; Lodes: 112; Salva Lopez, Studio Blanco: 102; Davide Lovatti, Arflex: 80; Mabeo Studio: 044; Emmanuele Maccio: 071; Constantin Meyer: 030; Constantin Meyer, Koelnmesse: 036; Constantin Meyer, Marco Moretto: 036; Nicolas Millet: 072; Blaise Misiek, Juli Daoust: 045; Monitillo1980: 109; Walter Monti: 024; Moooi: 089; Marco Moretto: 016; Mikkel Mortensen/Yellows Studio: 097, 098, 123, 124, 125; Alexis Narodetzky: 081; Negri Firman: 026; Nichetto Studio: 021, 078, 119, 132; Offecct: 025, 039; Alberto Parise, Nudesign Studio: 023; Tiziano Reguzzi: 114; Max Rommel: 084, 127; Salviati srl: 001, 002, 004; Anders Schønnemann: 069, 079; Nicho Södling, Massimo Gardone: 020; Jason Strong Photography: 032; Studio Blanco: 103, 104, 105, 107, 108, 122, 128, 130; Studio Blanco, Terzo Piano, Nichetto Studio: 137; Studio Eye/Paderni, Massimo Gardone: 031; Studio Kiwi Bravo: 091; Studio Pointer: 067; Studio Sancal, David Frutos: 096; Studio van Assendelft, Inga Powilleit Photography: 070, 131; Steffan

Sundström: 082, 083; Svenskt Tenn: 094; Svenskt Tenn, Marco Franceschin (Murano images): 093; Gregor Tietze, Stefan Gifthaler, Stefan Gergely: 111; Bernard Touillon, Ethimo: 066, 074, 116; Hironori Tsukue: 077; Riccardo Urnato: 118; Maria Wretblad, Saša Antić, Rubelli: 121; Max Zambelli with Art Direction by Palomba Serafini Associati: 095; ZaoZuo: 047; N. Zocchi, B. Brancato: 033.

Biography

Luca Nichetto was born in Venice in 1976, where his artistic talents were inspired by the famous Murano glassmaking industry, which employed members of his family. His career effectively started in his schooldays, where holidays were spent selling his designs to local factories, before he went on to study at the city's Istituto Statale d'Arte and then take a degree in industrial design at the local Università Iuav di Venezia (IUAV), graduating in 1998. The following year, he joined the Murano-based glassmaker Salviati, later becoming a product designer and consultant for lighting company Foscarini. He took the leap to setting up his own practice in the city, Nichetto Studio, in 2006. Five years later came another major turn in his career, when he moved to Stockholm, Sweden, to start his family and opened a second studio there, combining his Italian flair with the Swedish spirit of modernity and sustainability.

Over the years, Luca has served as art director for many international design brands and gained a reputation as a multidisciplinary designer. He has lectured and led workshops at several universities, including serving as a professor of design at the IUAV, and has sat on juries for various international design competitions. His work is often featured in prestigious exhibitions worldwide and has been the subject of retrospectives in cities including London, New York and Beijing. His highly researched, innovative projects have earned him an impressive array of international awards for designs that range from products, accessories and furniture to architecture, exhibition design and branding.

Acknowledgements

Luca Nichetto would like to thank everyone he crossed paths with on this creative journey, especially those who, through believing, trusting, critiquing, and even refusing to work together, enabled and motivated him to make Nichetto Studio grow and be internationally recognised.

A huge thanks to the entire team at Nichetto Studio, both current and former members, who have contributed in a huge way to all the great successes achieved so far. In addition, Luca wishes to extend a sincere thanks to his mom, his Åsa, his Jack and Liv, as well as the rest of the family for the unconditional support that they have always provided him in pursuing his dreams.

And as always, a special tribute to the first person who believed in him: his father, Paolo Nichetto.

Phaidon Press Limited
2 Cooperage Yard
London E15 2QR

Phaidon Press Inc.
65 Bleecker Street
New York, NY 10012

phaidon.com
First published 2022
© 2022 Phaidon Press Limited
Texts © 2022 Luca Nichetto, Max Fraser and Francesca Picchi

Max Fraser and Francesca Picchi have asserted their rights to be identified as the authors of this work in accordance with the Copyright, Designs and Patents Act 1988

ISBN 978 1 83866 324 7

A CIP catalogue record for this book is available from the British Library and the Library of Congress.

All rights reserved. No part of this publication may be reproduced, stored in a retrieval system or transmitted, in any form or by any means, electronic, mechanical, photocopying, recording or otherwise, without the written permission of Phaidon Press Limited.

Commissioning Editor: Emilia Terragni
Project Editor: Emma Barton
Production Controller: Sarah Kramer
Design: Henrik Nygren Design

Texts on pages 9–11, 58–60, 76–78, 114–116, 138–140, 192–194 and 210–212 translated from the Italian by Richard Sadleir.

Printed in China

The publisher would like to thank Vanessa Bird, Robert Davies, Rosanna Fairhead, Keun Kim Roland and Mandy Mackie for their contributions to this book.